Beware Dobermanns, Donkeys and Ducks

Beware Dobermanns, Donkeys and Ducks

Alexandra Bastedo

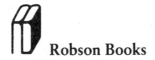

Robson Books

This Robson paperback edition first published in 1996.
First published in Great Britain in 1995 by Robson
Books Ltd, Bolsover House, 5–6 Clipstone Street,
London W1P 8LE

British Library Cataloguing in Publication Data
A catalogue record for this title is available from the
British Library

ISBN 0 86051 973 2 (hbk)
    1 86105 019 4 (pbk)

Printed by The Guernsey Press Company Ltd.,
Guernsey, Channel Islands

To my husband Patrick, Jessie, Jim and Bob, without whose tolerance, forbearance and endurance this book would not have been possible

PLAN OF POPLARS FARM

Contents

Acknowledgements

My thanks to Selsey architect Neil Mills for allowing me to reproduce his plan of Poplars as a frontispiece.

Warm thanks for all their advice to: Roger Sked, Ferret Rescue; Susan Luxford-Watts, Cornish Rex Rescue; Jimmy Gough, Donkey Rescue; Monique Turk, Cat, Rabbit and Guinea-Pig Rescue; Dennis Fenter, Brent Lodge Bird Hospital; Jo Gibbs, Di Patience and Liz Fitzgerald, Dobermann Rescue; Frank Page, the poultry fancier; David Bland, the poultry expert; Mark Luffman, the fish specialist; Downlands Vet and Allpress vets.

And thanks to all my neighbours for helping to recapture the fugitives and putting up with all the cacophony.

Introduction

It was when I discovered I could tell the health of a duck by the dark circles under its eyes that I realized how far I had come from life in Berkeley Square.

Not that life as an actress in Mayfair, with glamorous escorts and travelling on films to exotic locations, hadn't been exciting – it had. But my original ambition had been to be a vet. I had been deflected from this when, at the age of sixteen, I was sent to Hollywood by Columbia Pictures to make a film. At twenty I was the female star of the cult TV series *The Champions*; my childhood hobby, acting, had become my profession and my passion for animals had become my pastime.

After seventeen years of a nomadic life, jetting from continent to continent, however, the crisis finally came. It happened in my hotel room in New York at 2 o'clock one morning. A simple thing – I wanted to go to the bathroom but seemed incapable of finding the light switch. This confusion was enough to reduce me to floods of tears.

Up from filming in Central America to compère a fashion show at the Saint Régis hotel in New York, *en route* to my apartment in Toronto before flying on to Spain for a commercial, I became aware for the first time of the toll my turbulent lifestyle was taking on my nervous system. I determined to pack up my Canadian flat and head home for London.

Little did I know, but it was a decision that was to lead me to a rural oasis – a seventeenth-century farmhouse in deepest Sussex, surrounded by animals. A menagerie of dobermanns, donkeys and ducks, not to mention cats and chipmunks, hens and hares, geese, guinea-pigs and guinea-fowls, turkeys, ferrets and fish – and all their accompanying ailments.

I began as an amateur, barely able to distinguish between hay and straw, but rapidly grew into an expert who could diagnose with ease flukes, fin rot, foot root, seedy toe, scaly leg, black head, bots and bumble foot. At last I had stumbled upon my true vocation.

1

Early Stages

'I want to be the Elephant Lady,' I announced to my parents at the age of three after a visit to Billy Smart's Circus. They were amused at such childlike determination and were unaware that their daughter's combined passion for animals and love of show-business was manifesting itself at such a young age.

Or maybe it was in the genes: my mother, half Swiss, half Italian, had a Yugoslavian opera singer for an aunt, while her grandmother, Theresa Wagner, was a close relative of Richard Wagner; my father was an all-Canadian boy of Saskatchewan farming stock from the prairies who counted a Mohawk Princess named Ots-Toch among his ancestors. They met during the Second World War in Brighton, England.

'Can't we live in the country, Daddy?' I often pleaded. 'Then we could have some animals.'

'I've seen enough mud in the Canadian Army to last me a lifetime, pumpkin,' he would reply. 'I intend to live the rest of my life in towns, surrounded by pavements.' Mother wasn't much better, and the only walks she ever enjoyed were on the paved promenades of Worthing or Brighton seafronts.

My attempts at pet-keeping in my childhood were largely doomed. Our dachshund was given away because mother said she couldn't cope with a dog and three

1

children under five (I had a brother, Lindsay, and sister, Penny), and our cat was also found another home because Lindsay developed eczema.

Thus, with just a tiny garden at the back of the house, my pets were limited to Thumper the rabbit (so-called because he would escape from his run and thump on the coal bin outside our bedroom at daybreak each morning) and two tortoises, Spotty Dick and Minnie the Roamer. The former I dropped on concrete and his shell cracked, but I managed to save him with the help of Elastoplast; the latter lived up to her name and one day disappeared, never to be seen again.

At the local school I was considered somewhat lethargic in my studies, so when my parents were told there was little chance of their sluggish nine-year-old daughter passing the 11-plus exam, they devised an ill-conceived plan.

Thanks to my well-thumbed copy of *Black Beauty* and regular visits to the local riding stables, I had become horse-mad. 'If you pass your 11-plus this year we'll buy you a pony,' said my mother. My form teacher was stunned by the overnight change in personality of his dozy student, who now hung on his every word. I passed my 11-plus effortlessly and was now scholarship material.

'How can we keep a pony in our back garden?' said my father. I ignored such logic. 'You *said* I could have a pony,' I insisted, unwilling to relinquish my promised reward. Finally in an attempt to mollify me they proffered a black poodle puppy whose woolly coat would not affect my brother's allergy. Grudgingly I accepted, but Noddy, as I called him, was so inbred, neurotic, and had so many fits, that I think even my mother admitted in the end that a pony might have been easier. I was also taking Noddy frequently to the local veterinary surgeon and would help out there whenever I could. Soon I resolved to be a vet.

It was my mother who inadvertently started me on my dramatic career after a grammatical argument.

'I could of done it,' I had said, about something or other.

'I could *have* done it,' she corrected.

I insisted on the former. 'I could *of*,' I repeated.

'You,' she said, 'are going to elocution classes to learn how to speak.' Much to her surprise I took to them like a duck to water and started winning prizes in the local Worthing and Brighton Festivals. Soon after, I joined the Lewes Little Theatre amateur company, appearing in, among others, *The Tempest* and *View from the Bridge*. It was while I was playing Miss Matty in the amateur production of *Cranford*, a dramatization of Mrs Gaskell's book by A. A. Milne, that an advertisement to find 'The Teenage Diplomat for Great Britain' appeared in the *London Evening News*. The prize was a trip to Hollywood for the winner and her chaperone, and a part in *The Candy Web*, a film for Columbia Pictures. My mother filled in the form, enclosed a photograph of me looking like an English rose, and entered me for it.

A month later I found myself in the Wardour Street offices of Columbia Pictures auditioning in front of Anna Neagle, the actress; Maud Spector, a top casting director; Mike Frankovitch, head of Columbia Pictures; and C. R. Willis, the Editor of the *London Evening News*. I was extremely nervous but in my pocket I carried a special good luck charm: a greetings telegram which had arrived the previous evening from Miss Sweeting, my Latin teacher. It read: FELIX SIS CRAS ET REDEAS VICTRIX – 'May you be lucky tomorrow and return victorious'.

The audition consisted of sight-reading a piece from *Sabrina Fair* and an interview. What subjects was I studying? they wanted to know. What did I want to do with my life? I told them about my acting at school and about a recent venture into directing (my *Pride and Prejudice* had just won the school Inter-House competition) but, perhaps wisely, I neglected to mention my lurking veterinary ambitions.

Whether it was my new genteel accent, my acting ability, or my hybrid 'English rose' looks that influenced the judges I don't know, but shortly after my interview I was informed that I had won – out of four thousand applicants.

Only two weeks after that I was in Hollywood – staying in a five-star hotel, being driven around in limousines and being introduced to real live movie stars: Charlton Heston, Ty Hardin, Sandra Dee, Ann-Margret, even the young Omar Sharif, fresh from making *Dr Zhivago*. It was enough to turn any young girl's head and it turned mine.

The part I'd won was in a film called *The Candy Web*, directed by William Castle (who went on to produce *Rosemary's Baby*). It was a pretty second-rate horror film, full of people on meat-hooks in refrigerators, but I had a fair number of lines interspersed with screams, gasps and looks of wide-eyed terror. When my four weeks' work ended Columbia paid me several hundred dollars. Not many young people in England earned that much in a year. I returned home to Brighton suddenly aware that I might actually be able to make a living from something I had previously thought of as just a hobby.

One of the dividends of winning the competition was that I acquired an agent, and straight after my return he started to send me amazing offers. Would I do a TV series in Hollywood with Donna Reed? Would I make a film, *The Girl in Blue Jeans* for Alfred Hitchcock? Yes of course I would. 'Oh no, you won't,' chorused my parents.

'You are only sixteen and you have to finish your education. You have your A levels to take and then university. Besides which, your headmistress will expel you if you take any more time off.'

I was appalled. How could A levels compare with the glamorous life I'd just sampled? What sort of parents would sabotage a daughter's career like that? My new-found sophistication evaporated and I regressed to screaming tantrums, but it was no good. They pointed out that they had two other children to think of and, after seeing the temptations of Hollywood at first hand, my mother had no intention of letting me go alone. So back to school I went. It was, in retrospect, the right decision, but I have always regretted the lost opportunity to be directed by Hitchcock. The prospect of another nine years' study to be a vet held no appeal now and I gave up science and spent my sixth-form years studying French, English and Latin. Despite my rather grudging approach I passed all three and was offered places at both Manchester and London Universities. But the seeds sown two years earlier had taken root and I wanted no more of study. The day after I left school for the last time I rang my agent and told him I was available for acting work. Shortly afterwards he rang back.

'How would you like to do a part in *The Count of Monte Cristo* for BBC television?' I told him I would like it very much. It marked the end of my academic life.

My childhood dream of living in the country surrounded by animals was put on the back burner. Film and television work was centred on London and if I wanted to succeed as an actress that was where I would have to live. I moved into a basement flat in Earls Court with two other girls from Hove and for the next few months my life became an endless round of auditions.

Compared with today there seemed to be plenty of

acting work available: American companies were making fifty films a year in Britain; TV series were plentiful, and the theatre was thriving. So I didn't have the uphill struggle my parents had predicted. After *The Count of Monte Cristo*, jobs came one after the other, mostly small TV parts at first; I appeared in four episodes of *Compact*, a television soap, then did a TV comedy series with Harry Worth.

After eighteen months I landed my first film part – a small role in the spoof James Bond film *Casino Royale*, where I had to play opposite Peter Sellers as a blonde and then adopt a red wig and a heavy Scottish accent to seduce David Niven. David proved to be just as charming in life as on film. One day as we waited around on set he informed me that we were both introverts because we were born under Pisces. It was certainly true as far as I was concerned – I was desperately reserved as a teenager and not very talkative at all – but I found it hard to believe that the urbane David suffered from similar shyness.

While filming *Casino Royale* I met another young actress, Nicole Shelby and by now we were both earning enough to move into a flat in Knightsbridge. It was a great relief as, since leaving my seedy flat in Earls Court, I had been sharing an icy top-floor flat with Australian girls who partied all night and invited streams of visiting relatives to sleep on the floor. Nicole was a vast improvement as a flat-mate as she, like me, was aware of the perils of turning up to auditions with dark rings under your eyes.

One day our curiosity was aroused when one of the executive producers brought Warren Beatty on to the set and introduced him to all the pretty actresses. That same night Nicole and I were sound asleep in our shared bedroom in our flat in Knightsbridge when, at one in the morning, the telephone went. My bed was nearest to it, so I answered.

'Hi, Alexandra –' there was a distinct American accent – 'this is Warren here, I'm all alone and I wondered if you would like to come over for a drink?' 'Thank you very much, Mr Beatty, but I'm sound asleep, goodnight,' I said, and stumbled back into bed. At 3 a.m. the phone went again and, once again, it was me who staggered over . . .

'Hi, Nicole –' I detected the same unmistakable American accent – 'this is Warren here, I'm all alone and I wondered . . .' Poor Warren Beatty. He had obviously got hold of the producer's address book and worked his way frustratedly through the alphabet of English actresses. I was B for Bastedo and by the time he reached Nicole, who was S for Shelby, it was three in the morning and he'd still had no luck!

Sometimes life seems to turn full circle: on a recent trip to Los Angeles I was having lunch with a Californian girlfriend and at the end of the meal she said: 'There is something I have been wanting to tell you for a long time – when you stayed with me eleven years ago there was a telephone call for you, after you left, from Warren Beatty. When I told him you had just departed for England he said, "Who are *you*, and why don't you come over for a drink?" I was intrigued,' she told me, 'and decided to play a little hard to get. I said I would think about it and he said he would ring back in half an hour to see if I had changed my mind. In that half an hour I bathed, washed my hair and doused myself in perfume and waited coolly for the phone to ring. Sure enough it did, on the dot of nine o'clock. "Have you changed your mind?" Warren said. "Well . . ." This time I let myself be persuaded by his dulcet tones and off I went in a cab to his apartment. And do you know I didn't leave for three whole days, he was wonderful! Unfortunately,' she said, 'he never rang me again, but do you know I never regretted a minute of it!'

Despite all the glamorous work and escorts, I missed the company of animals. Some evenings, letting myself into the empty flat after a long day's filming, I'd even feel quite nostalgic about poor Noddy, the neurotic poodle. I tried to fill the void by collecting fish, and soon the flat was filled with gurgling tanks of shubunkins, fantails, blackamoors and baby koi carp; but though nice to look at, I found them fairly unrewarding companions. I was therefore delighted when a friend gave me a tiny Yorkshire terrier. I christened him Huston after John Huston, the larger-than-life director of *Casino Royale*. I had never been particularly attracted to small dogs but Huston was far from being a lap-dog: he was farm-bred from working terrier parents which meant he was not only intelligent – refusing for example, to cross the road except at zebra crossings – but was also very bold.

One benefit of Huston's size was that I was often able to smuggle him into the studios, but occasionally I would ask Nicole to dog-sit and she was so captivated by Huston that she decided to acquire a Yorkshire terrier of her own, which she called Charlie. Unfortunately Charlie was bred for the show ring and was as stupid as Huston was bright, bounding headlong into traffic and totally refusing to be house-trained. When we took them on country walks, Huston would carefully skirt puddles and ditches, but Charlie would plunge in blindly and look totally taken aback at finding himself drenched to the skin. The two dogs enjoyed each other's company, though I think Huston always regarded Charlie as a rather slow-witted relative.

Then, when I was twenty, along came a job that not

only brought me the success I coveted but taught me all about its down side too. *The Champions* was a filmed television series of thirty hour-long episodes: an escapist fantasy about two men and a woman who had been in a plane crash in Tibet and were rescued by a group of other-worldly people. When the three heroes (played by William Gaunt, Stuart Damon and me) regained consciousness, they found that, thanks to the attention of these mystics, they had abnormal powers of strength, hearing, sight, smell and telepathy. They put these to use working for an organization called Nemesis, whose mission was to seek out evil-doers like drug smugglers and Russian spies.

Filming the thirty episodes took a year and three months and was a tremendous experience. There were guest actors in most episodes and to find myself working with people like Jeremy Brett (whom I'd hero-worshipped since I'd seen him play Hamlet during a school theatre trip) was an extraordinary feeling. However, I had never worked so hard in my life. The day started at six when I gave my hair its obligatory daily shampoo: at seven-thirty sharp I arrived at the studio for make-up: by eight-thirty I was on set. We worked every other Saturday, and on my Saturdays 'off' I was carted round the shops looking for suitable clothes for my character, Sharron Macready. Sometimes we'd be filming two or three episodes at a time on different sets and I hardly knew what the story was. The tight schedule meant I had to be extremely self-disciplined and wave goodbye to any kind of social life.

It also meant, since no dogs were allowed on the set, and Nicole had gone to America, that I had to give Huston to my parents for a year. I missed him dreadfully, and towards the end of the series I started to feel really down, mentally and physically, and developed a severe throat infection. I soldiered on, but the moment the series finished I was taken into hospital to have my tonsils out.

I felt exhausted for quite a while afterwards and I didn't even have Huston to cheer me up since – understandably after fifteen months – my parents had become too attached to him to hand him back. But when after several delays *The Champions* was shown I was more than compensated. Overnight the series achieved cult status, and William, Stuart and I became celebrities. People recognized me in the street, I was asked to open fêtes and supermarkets, and I received fan mail from all over the world.

Most of the letters were straightforward, but others were disturbing. Some people seemed to confuse me with my character Sharron Macready and wrote as if I were the one with telepathic powers. ('I know I don't have to tell you this, Alexandra, because you already know what I'm thinking . . .') Others made the not-unusual assumptions about actresses: finding myself the object of men's fantasies was quite an eye-opener. I may have been twenty-one but I'd led a sheltered life and I was still rather naive. I received a polite letter from a sailor requesting a photo of me in high-heeled shoes – with a postscript asking me to include the shoes as well! Then there was the American Indian who wrote saying he'd left his tepee to me in his will, and the professor who wrote me a long love poem nearly every day, which the TV studio dutifully forwarded.

With friends I laughed it off but secretly I found people like the professor a bit scary. How could he get so obsessive about someone he didn't even know? Other aspects of fame frightened me too: I had a horrible experience opening a fête in Yorkshire, when I was mobbed and had to be rescued by police.

Since filming *The Champions* I'd been going out with

the actor Anthony Valentine, who was quite concerned I might be a target for a psychopath. I didn't take his worries too seriously at first but then something happened to make me think again. Tony was appearing at The Theatre Royal, Brighton with Linda Thorsen who had starred in another cult TV series, *The Avengers*, and had also been deluged with fan-mail. One evening Tony heard sounds of a scuffle in Linda's dressing room, and ran in to find a man threatening to stab her. Luckily he overpowered the man before he could do any harm, but the incident made him more anxious for my safety, especially as I was due to start a tour of provincial theatres.

'You're going to have to think about security, Alex,' he insisted. 'Your movements are predictable when you're appearing on stage.' It was true. Any mad professor who looked up the performance times could work out what time I'd be leaving the stage door. It was a chilling thought, but I didn't see how I could lessen the risk. My anxiety grew worse two weeks before the tour when my flat was broken into and my modest collection of antique snuffboxes and some jewellery I'd bought with the money from *The Champions* were stolen. Suddenly I felt very vulnerable and insecure. It was Tony who came up with a solution.

'Why don't you get yourself another dog, Alex?' he suggested. 'A proper dog this time –' Tony had always been rather scathing about little Huston – 'one that'll stand up for you if you find yourself in a fix.'

'What do you mean by a proper dog?' I asked warily.

Tony smiled. 'There's only one breed I'd call a proper dog,' he said. 'What you need is a dobermann pinscher.'

2

Me, You and a Dog Named Blue

'I'm thinking of getting a dobermann,' I said at breakfast to my friend Ruth with whom I was staying in Cardiff on the tour of *Conduct Unbecoming*.

'The wish is father to the deed,' said Ruth enigmatically. It just so happened that one of her neighbours, Mrs Evans, bred dobermann pinschers, they had recently had a litter and she happened to have one left.

At noon I was at the Evans'. 'He's the runt, I'm afraid,' said Mrs Evans, 'but he's got a lovely nature, just like his mother. You can see her if you like.'

'There's no need,' I replied guardedly, unwilling to admit that while I wasn't afraid of her sweet, dachshund-like slobbering puppy I wasn't too keen on meeting his large relatives at all. I had seen far too many horror films featuring snarling dobermanns and I couldn't associate this little creature with enormous paws sitting on my lap with them at all. I looked into his adoring brown eyes and was lost, I took a deep breath, and –

'I'll have him, Mrs Evans,' I said.

On the drive back we heard on the car-radio a song, 'Me, You, and a Dog Named Blue' and that is what he was called. Later I found out the song was really 'Me, You, and a Dog Named Boo'. It was a happy mistake as Blue really suited him, with his shiny blue-black coat, whereas 'Boo' for a dobermann would have been plain silly!

Blue spent his formative months touring round the country with me and the cast of *Conduct Unbecoming*, visiting twenty-one actors from dressing room to dressing room back stage. I always tried to stay in small country hotels where there would be somewhere to walk him, and such was his puppyish charm that often the proprietors would leave dinner for both of us after the performance. Outside Glasgow in the Campsie Fells Blue so beguiled the waitress at the Campsie Glen Hotel that she would take him for an early morning walk each day, leaving me to enjoy a lazy breakfast in bed. At Newcastle we would go for long bracing runs along Hadrian's Wall, I was fitter than I had ever been and Blue no longer resembled a dachshund, but looked like a slightly chunky greyhound.

At the final date, Aberdeen, a letter was handed to me, it said: 'Dear Alexandra, I saw your green eyes flashing towards me in the third row last night, but you came out of the stage door with your dobermann, so I didn't dare approach you.' It was signed 'The Professor'. Blue had won his spurs just by being himself, walking at my side. He was now the classic example of a fully fledged black and tan dobermann.

As a result of the touring, Blue grew to love people and to adore travelling, and if ever he was anywhere longer than a week, he would soon get restless, then bored, and then he'd begin to misbehave.

Having a large dog in London is a liability and they must be well-trained. Luckily, because of the occasional 'resting' period, I was able to spend a lot of time on him: he walked impeccably to heel, fetched and carried on command and when he came to the hairdresser's, contentedly chewed curlers on the floor until it was time to leave. He was a well-known figure all around Mayfair and the West End; Allen's the famous butcher's even kept aside tasty morsels for him on our frequent trips up Mount Street which, naturally, became his favourite walk. Living in a flat, however, was not ideal: early risers would see me with a coat over my nightie in Berkeley Square, and once a day we would go for a very long walk in Hyde Park, but during those years in Mayfair as a single girl I dread to think how I would have fared without him. At the age of six months, he gave chase to thieves who were stealing my car, and at the age of a year, he saw off a man who was pestering me in the park and although I was burgled often it was never when Blue was in residence.

Brought up, as he was, in London, he could never stop being a town dog; when we were in the countryside he would ignore all the wonderful smells of the rabbits and foxes, and demand that you threw his ball all the time and if you went indoors he would press his nose against the glass and beseech you to let him in – gardens and woods without his toys held no attraction. There was only one country pastime he really enjoyed and that was hauling the most enormous logs. This later prompted my little godson, Simon Mulligan, while watching a production of the York Mystery Plays to whisper to me as they hauled up Christ's great wooden cross, 'Blue would have liked that.'

The police don't use dobermanns because they maintain that whenever they issue a command, alsatians obey instantly, whereas dobermanns think about it, and have to decide whether the order is a good one before acting on it. Whenever Blue misbehaved, I always had one means of blackmail at my disposal. Living in such a busy, congested part of London, I felt a monthly need to get rid of the grime in Blue's coat when it began to look lacklustre; so I would fill a bath full of foam bubbles, lift his rigid body into it and wash him in Johnson's baby shampoo, which cleansed him without hurting him, while he reproached me with baleful brown eyes. So much did he dread his monthly torture that in any situation requiring good behaviour all I had to do was call out 'Bath', and he was instant obedience and docility.

After *Conduct Unbecoming* I experienced for the first time the phenomenon of 'resting' between jobs, which is often difficult to cope with. However, Tony had been an actor from his childhood and had become expert on what to do with his time when not working, and he taught me quite simply that if you spend a day happily listening to lovely music or looking at beautiful paintings or just walking the dog, then that is a day valuably spent. Maybe the reason why so many people are workaholics and feel guilty when not working is that they are unable to enjoy their free time.

Tony also introduced me to his two great passions, scuba-diving and mountain climbing. The former we did in Cyprus, in Kyrenia, and diving enabled me to meet all the octopuses, lobsters and fish at first hand, particularly as I would take down handfuls of Ryvita with me to feed them and would quickly find myself surrounded by shoals of colourful fish. However, if ever I found myself near Andreas, our instructor, I would stop as, armed with his spear gun, he would be searching for our lunch to cook on board! You could tell an octopus's lair by the variety of stones placed outside its hole; they have such bad digestive systems that their intelligence tells them to use a small stone to push a tiny fish down their gullet, and a large stone to force down a big one. It's hardly surprising that marine biologists find their species highly advanced. Equally clever were the lobsters who seem the friendliest of creatures, very family-orientated, and responsible in their relationships, walking miles to see uncles and aunts, and very protective of their wives in the moulting season. Our dives were restricted to one hundred and twenty feet which was the safety margin with an aqualung and no decompression chamber, but I longed to encounter the creatures that dwell at greater depths.

Tony's other passion, mountain climbing, was able to include Blue, although with me in tow it was more like fell-walking, particularly in the Lake District. On these occasions Blue would lose his disciplined London personality, plunging headlong into icy pools and scaling slippery rock faces. His look of astonishment as gravity came into play and he slipped backwards with his claws splayed outwards like a cartoon cat would have us in fits of laughter. However, nothing fazed him and he was always ready to confront the next crag. At night, back at our little pub in Ullswater, after a hearty meal, he would curl up in front of the open fire and snore contentedly, re-living his adventures of the day.

Some months later I was invited to replace Joanna Lumley in *Don't Just Lie There, Say Something* a Brian Rix farce, at the Garrick Theatre, and accepted, primarily in order to live the same hours as Tony Valentine who was starring in *Sleuth* at the Wyndham's Theatre just up the road.

However, by now, sadly, after three and a half years Tony and I were beginning to go our own ways. The pressures of being an actor and actress together had taken their toll. When we were both out of work we were miserable – when we were both working on different locations around the world we hardly saw each other; neither extreme was a recipe for happiness, no matter how fond we were of each other.

One day depressed by the split-up, and the prospect of my approaching thirtieth birthday, I happened to bump into Omar Sharif in a little hotel just off Bond Street.

'Alexandra, it is your birthday,' he said. 'I must take you to dinner.' Looking into his limpid brown eyes who was I to refuse?

Two weeks later he had lunch with William Hall from the *Evening Standard*, and the next day to my amazement I read of our formal engagement on the front page of the newspaper. This was shortly followed by our photograph on the cover of America's *National Enquirer*! This prompted a Californian friend to send a caustic telegram: 'What's this I hear about you and some Arab!' Needless to say, that relationship was destined to come to a swift end in spite of all of Omar's exceptional charm. I was unable to survive the endless evenings while he played bridge, the appalling late nights (or early mornings) and, most of all, the procession of beautiful women surreptitiously stuffing their telephone numbers into his top pocket. Omar was enormously attractive, but he was not exclusive!

Shortly afterwards I was photographed holding hands with David Frost at the film première of *The Great Gatsby*, and it had the desired effect: immediately the press stopped linking me with Omar, and at the same time ceased going on about David's broken engagement to the American model, Karen Graham.

However, in spite of all the attention to my personal life, the largest amount of publicity I ever received was to be over Blue.

The Champions had been a huge hit in Spain as *Los Invincibiles de Nemesis* and that, together with my Spanish surname and the fact that I spoke French, Italian and Spanish, resulted in my making twelve Spanish coproductions over ten years. I won two awards and became known to the Spaniards, flatteringly, as 'La Bastedo'.

The films provided a necessary income and it was a wonderful way to get to know Spain, spending six weeks at a time in various locations. However, it did have one major draw-back: I couldn't take Blue with me because of Britain's quarantine laws. For the first few trips I left Blue with Tony as my mother couldn't have him. Huston, the Yorkie, would try to savage poor bewildered Blue, who would never touch him. When Tony and I parted, an old schoolfriend of my brother's, Ronald, who worked nearby on Bond Street offered to dog-sit and this I gratefully accepted.

Ronald loved Blue, even taking him to his office every day, and Blue in return adored Ronald. As he was in the same area it meant Blue was still taken on his usual walks, so his life didn't alter radically while I was away filming.

A few weeks later when I was offered a part in a Canadian television series, Ronald said he would foster Blue for me.

Working in Canada wasn't an option for most English actresses but thanks to my Canadian father I had dual nationality. Canada had a relatively small film and television industry at that time, and it was a wonderful surprise to find that I was a big fish in a small pond and soon in great demand. In a relatively short while I was offered films opposite the major Canadian stars of that time; I called Ronald in London who assured me that Blue showed no sign of pining, and that he was quite happy to continue as foster parent, and wouldn't even mind if I accepted the offer to star in two productions at the Shaw Festival Theater, Niagara-on-the-Lake, for six months. The town, beautifully preserved, is set amongst farms in the wine growing area. Every evening I would leave my little cottage, tuck my make-up bag in my wicker basket, and bicycle off at a leisurely pace to play on alternate nights either Lady Mary in *The Admirable Crichton* at the large Shaw Theater, or Raina in *Arms and the Man* at the old Court House Theater. It was idyllic, as this was the first time I had achieved my ambition of living, as well as working, in the country.

When I finally returned to England I was quite prepared for Ronald to tell me that he didn't want to give Blue back (as my parents had with Huston). What I wasn't prepared for was the news that Ronald had been caught between two warring girlfriends and had given one of them my dog in an attempt to appease her. My brother Lindsay knew the girl, who had formerly rented a room in his flat. The outlook was extremely worrying. He revealed that every day she locked Blue in her room from eight in the morning until six at night while she was at work all through that exceptionally hot summer. She hardly ever exercised him and his feeding hours were erratic.

I was distraught and racked with guilt over Blue, and wondered how on earth I could possibly get him back. I consulted a lawyer friend.

'Don't quote me,' he said, 'but possession is nine-tenths of the law. It will take you a year or more to get him back if you go through the courts.'

There was only one thing to be done and I planned a secret campaign worthy of the SAS. First I found out where the girl would be walking Blue on a particular day and then lay in wait in jeans and running shoes. When they finally appeared, Blue was on the lead, which had never been necessary with me as he had always remained glued to my heel. I ran up without warning and swiftly removed the choke chain which left Blue both leadless and collarless. He was so overjoyed to see me that as I sprinted towards the park exit, he of course came too. There a good friend had his Porsche revving in gear with the door open, and we jumped in and accelerated towards Brighton and my parents' house, Blue's favourite place. When we arrived and took him for a walk on the beach we were both appalled at his condition; he could hardly put one foot in front of the other, his skin was scurvy, and it was to be months before he was back to normal.

The very next day I was due to leave to shoot a short film in Madrid and was astounded when, as I was going through Heathrow Passport Control, a gentleman stepped out and said:

'Miss Bastedo? will you please step this way.' I was under arrest for stealing back *my* dog. I told the police what a stupid mistake they were making and explained the circumstances, but the woman had taken out a Court Order, and evidently the police were obliged to carry it out. I was driven to Savile Row Police Station, fingerprinted, photographed, and formally charged with stealing a dobermann – I did point out to the police that no one in their right mind would steal a *strange* dobermann, but they didn't see the joke! Fortunately my lawyer, Albion Gee, came to the rescue, assisted by a rather formidable crime specialist barrister. I was released on £100 bail the following day after appearing before the judge, and when they had ascertained that Blue was safely in Hove with my mother I was allowed to leave for Spain. By now, ironically, Huston had been killed, having taken on one labrador too many, so Mother and Father were very happy to take care of him.

The following morning when I arrived back at Heathrow, the photographers pounced, and the next day almost every newspaper in Britain carried the story. Two of the more imaginative headlines were: 'Actress Sees Red Over Blue' and 'Alex Pinches Pinscher'. By accident Blue had occasioned me more publicity than any one of my former celebrity escorts.

While I was in Spain it was established without doubt

that I was the rightful owner and the case was sensibly abandoned. It was an interesting experience, though not one I would ever care to repeat.

Over the next few months, with good food and regular exercise, Blue regained his stamina and the sheen on his blue-black coat. According to the vet his symptoms were simply those of neglect.

The whole experience filled me with guilt and I realized that as an itinerant actress it had been selfish and irresponsible of me to take on a pet without having someone permanent to leave him with. At least now when I was away, poor Huston being dead, Blue would always be with my parents in Brighton and no one else.

Through the whole nightmarish experience Blue had made friends too. That Christmas, from Savile Row Police Station, Blue received a greeting card; it read:

'To Blue,
   Happy Christmas,
     from
       The Boys in Blue'.

3

Love Me Love My Dog

'Love me love my dog' goes the song; in my case it was
love me, love my dobermann. Most potential admirers
would normally have to pass muster with one's mother,
but, before they ever got to meet my parents, hopeful
suitors would have to run the gauntlet of Blue. And it
wasn't just a case of them liking *him* – he was my protector, my trusted companion, and he had to take to them
too.

On reflection, a single girl with a dobermann that slept
at the end of her bed must have been a slightly daunting
prospect. When people rang the bell outside they would
be greeted by a very deep-throated bark, although upon
their being ushered into the flat Blue would exhibit a certain guarded shyness while he summed them up. Of
course, ironically, the more uneasy people were the less
likely he was to approve them. The second visit was even
more perturbing, as Blue would recognize the guests,
welcome them in the hall, clamping his jaws firmly
around their wrist, and pull them determinedly into the
living room. There weren't many people who enjoyed
having their Turnbull and Asser shirt-cuffs slobbered
over, but some realized that it was a compliment, as it
meant they had been accepted by Blue.

However, it must be said that Blue did put off a
number of would-be suitors. There was the young man

of peerless lineage I met on a flight from Spain, for instance. He was the hunting, shooting, fishing type that believed dogs should live in outside kennels, and he thoroughly disapproved of Blue. Blue sensed this and would growl menacingly whenever he tried to come near me. In fact it would be true to say that Blue literally saw him off! One person who passed the 'Blue test' with flying colours was my husband-to-be, director Patrick Garland. Patrick has such a sunny, confident, disposition that I don't think it would ever have occurred to him that any person or any dog, be it rottweiler, dobermann or alsatian, would not approve of him. Thus when he first met Blue at my flat he greeted him as a long-lost friend and Blue's little stump of a tail wagged away and he spent the evening glued to Patrick's side looking up at him with adoring eyes. Blue's mistress, it has to be said, was somewhat taken with Patrick as well.

We had met earlier, pre-Tony Valentine and pre-Blue, at the one hundredth performance of *Brief Lives* which Patrick had directed and adapted, with Roy Dotrice as the seventeenth-century antiquary, John Aubrey. He was the youngest director at that time to have three productions running concurrently in the West End of London and I had the good fortune to be seated next to him at dinner. With his penetrating blue eyes, mop of bohemian hair, and beautifully modulated voice I fell quickly under his spell.

A month later we went to Ireland together in Patrick's gunmetal blue SL 190 Mercedes, even in those days a collector's item. However, I was quickly to learn that for all Patrick's artistry and erudition he was totally impractical. The exhaust pipe was held on by a leather trouser-belt, and rain poured in through the passenger window which was jammed firmly open. These discomforts apart, the trip was magical: in Bantry Bay we hired a boat to Clear

Island to see the spectacular bird sanctuary, and at Ardnaside, in the Ring of Kerry, we went boating and rode horses over the heather-clad hills. I also noticed that Patrick's suitcase contained very few clothes, just masses of books and I soon learnt that Patrick read books like people smoked cigarettes, as an addiction. (He maintains he doesn't remember doing much reading on that particular trip!) The intensity of our passion was never in dispute, but we were both young, both too ambitious perhaps and the romance didn't last. Perhaps, at that time, it was not intended to. We both went on to other projects, and other relationships, but throughout them, wherever we were in the world, and whoever we were with, we remained friends and corresponded regularly.

In order to cope with my frenetic, nomadic schedule I was at one time maintaining a flat in Mayfair, an apartment in Madrid, and a condominium in Toronto and, filling in a questionnaire for British Airways one day, I surprised myself when I worked out that I was on a plane approximately every ten days. It wasn't a situation that was conducive to a stable emotional life and though the travelling was exciting, the jet-lag was exhausting.

At the peak of all this activity I landed in Costa Rica to make the film *Tu Dios, Mi Infierno*, a Spanish-Central American co-production; and never was *Your God, My Hell* more aptly named. Disaster first struck when we arrived in Costa Rica with the impounding of all the camera equipment by customs officials. However, our enforced inactivity was more than rewarded by the fact that it was carnival week in San José, and from our rooms at the Grand Hotel where we were on stand-by in case the equipment was suddenly released my co-star John Phillip Law, Fernando Arribas, the camera man, and I had a first-class view of the spectacular processions.

All too soon the equipment was released and the daily nightmare of *Tu Dios, Mi Infierno* commenced. The Costa Ricans could not fathom the meaning of continuity, no matter how many times it was explained to them. Thus you might start driving down the road in a white car and arrive at the destination next day in a red one, all because Juan Antonio, the owner of the white car, had gone to a night club and was too hung-over to turn up.

Another sequence had John Phillip Law water-skiing behind the motor-boat I was driving. When he fell into the sea, there were screams of 'Tiburón! Tiburón!' ('Shark! Shark!'); no one had told us we were filming in shark-infested waters. Luckily John was a very strong swimmer. Further escapades included our being turned into the street by the owners of the house in which we were filming as some unexpected guests had arrived early for Christmas. Another time the locals chopped down the electricity poles in revolt at the number of car accidents there had been. This left us with no electricity, and a generator from the American Army Base was brought in. That night instead of petrol, some other combustible fluid was poured into this very expensive piece of equipment, and it exploded. The next morning we fled the country.

Our arrival in Panama augured little better. At our hotel I asked the receptionist what the exact time was: 'There is no such thing as *exact* time in Panama,' she said. Nor was there. Boats we went to catch according to the timetable didn't exist, and then inexplicably two boats would turn up which were not scheduled at all. This lack of logic applied to all forms of transport, so our filming was totally unpredictable. The final straw, however, was the reaction of the Bishop of Panama who managed to get a copy of our erotic script, and banned us from filming in his churches. This news threw our extremely pious Spanish director into a fit of hysterics: 'I'm a good Catholic, I love God, my script is religious, Santa Madonna,' he sobbed through his tears. The next day we were on a plane again, sneaking back into Costa Rica. By now, having got the measure of our film producers, John Phillip Law and I insisted on our personal belongings travelling with us on the scheduled aircraft, while the costumes were sent on a small chartered plane. Some camera equipment managed to end up in New York, and our costumes were left behind on the tarmac because the little plane was overloaded, and the cases subsequently lost or stolen. With me the situation could be remedied, but finding a priest's surplice for John, who is extremely tall was impossible as Costa Rican sacerdotes are not known for their height. When the cameras came back they filmed a whole sequence with him immobilized semi-naked behind the altar as the surplice only reached his waist. At this time too, all the actors went on strike sitting on the steps of the hotel refusing to work, as none of us had been paid. Fortunately the ruse worked and we finished our erratic Central American schedule. At last only one scene remained and this they decided to shoot later in Madrid. Another pointless exercise, as they discovered upon arrival that the Madrid countryside in winter, with bare trees and snow-covered terrain, bore little resemblance to equatorial Costa Rica. In retrospect it all seems very comical, but at the time we were all exhausted by the long hours and stressful conditions. I caught the first plane to New York where I was due to host a fashion show at the Saint Régis Hotel. It was there, while I tossed and turned fretfully, trying to come to terms with yet *another* time change and yet *another* hotel room that I couldn't discover the light switch. It was all that was needed to push me over the edge. I just disintegrated, tears coursing down my face, and sobbed helplessly.

What was I doing thousands of miles from home, away from my family, my friends and my beloved Blue? Jets, luxurious five-star hotels and colourful locations no longer held any appeal. Something had to be done about it before I went under completely. I flew back to Toronto, packed up my apartment, cancelled my Spanish commercial and headed back to England for Christmas.

Once back I called Patrick Garland and we arranged to meet. He had just finished a liaison of some three years standing with an ebullient Californian girlfriend who had gone back to Los Angeles in search of sunshine and transcendental meditation.

I suppose, in your youth, it's very easy to meet the right person at the wrong time. Each highly determined, Patrick and I had first met when I was twenty-one, he a decade older, and within a short time, recognizing the serious potential of the relationship, both of us fled in opposite directions. Timing is everything, and we were extremely lucky in a way to have met again thirteen years later, both still unattached. However, having said that, extracting a marriage proposal out of Patrick (who was a confirmed bachelor by then) proved harder than taking out an impacted wisdom tooth. I would drop hints from time to time, which were mainly met with gales of laughter. When I was offered a further television series in Canada however, even he realized it was no longer a joking matter.

'If you come with me to Corsica on holiday, you might find it could be worth your while,' Patrick insinuated heavily, for such an eloquent man strangely incapable of putting the correct and traditional words together. We did go to Corsica – to his little villa perched on a mountain top and overlooking the sea; his poetic description of Sant'Antonino as a village in the clouds, sounded enticing enough, a positive paradise, but after a week of

raging hurricanes which shook the house to its foundations, I felt as though we were living in *Wuthering
Heights*, and, there being no sign of a proposal, I began
to want to go home. But suddenly the fierce winds
dropped, the sun crept out from behind Mount Asco and
the beauty of La Balagne emerged, with its incredible
mountain views, transparent seas, and an air scented
with wild thyme and rosemary, and, as we picnicked on
Asco's glittering crest Patrick, most romantically – and at
last – asked me if I would consent to be his wife. I did.

Blue approved, mother and father approved, everyone
was happy. The only object of dispute was the venue:
mother wanted us to marry in Hove, and we wanted a
small wedding at the beautiful Westerham Parish Church
near Patrick's ragstone cottage on the Kentish Weald.
However, the situation was resolved when Patrick was
invited to be the Artistic Director of the Chichester
Festival Theatre, and the Bishop, Eric Kemp, and his
wife, Pat, very kindly offered us the Cathedral of the
Holy Trinity for the ceremony (as we were now residents) and the beautiful Bishop's Palace for our
reception.

The ceremony was presided over by our good friend
the Chancellor, Canon Roger Greenacre, and Patrick, in
his role as director as well as bridegroom had compiled a
beautiful service. I felt jittery, of course, and Patrick
looked ash-grey, but happiness and a sense of relief were
the predominant feelings, and after fourteen years of
knowing one another, at last we had made it to the altar!

After an all-too-brief honeymoon of three days and
nights in Brittany under snow, our priority was to collect
Blue from my parents and move into the elegant
eighteenth-century house we rented temporarily in The
Pallants, the Georgian quarter of Chichester.

The problem about being Director of the Chichester Theatre is that it's the job everyone wants, until they get it – then they discover it is the job *nobody* wants! The elegance of the place, the friendliness of the people who work there deceives the eye. Chichester seethes with hidden problems. Patrick immediately went to work to resolve his first crisis: typically, during our honeymoon, he had lost his first play of the season, Solzhenitsyn's *The Love Girl and the Innocent* (a genuinely courageous first production) and he needed an instant replacement. This was eventually to be Chekhov's *The Cherry Orchard*, starring Claire Bloom as Madame Ranyevska, to be adapted by Philip Roth.

While this was going on I set about finding our first marital home. We wanted it to be our dream come true, and we had both agreed that it would be a profound joy to live, as well as work, in the country. And in Sussex too. I was always a Worthing and Hove girl and, as a small child, Patrick had lived in a tumbledown medieval cottage in Rogate churchyard that his parents had rented. It is a part of England rich in poetic images, Blake's 'sweetest spot on earth'; best of all we were moving to Kipling country, to the 'Manhood' area south of Chichester, near the sea, as featured in my favourite poem, appropriately with a donkey and an ox, 'Eddi's Service'.

'Let us always remember this moment,' I said to Patrick as we surveyed Poplars Farm House for the first time. It was an absolute picture postcard: a seventeenth-century house, which with a thatched converted cowshed, stables and an old tithe barn, formed a collection of buildings as pretty as a Morland painting.

This I instinctively knew was my oasis, the home in the country I had often dreamed about. Fortunately,

Patrick too was entranced; not only was the setting idyllic, and only eight miles from the theatre, but the old thatched cowshed would make a perfect library for his precious books, about four thousand of them, and increasing all the time.

On top of that, Patrick's poor mother, Rosalind, had just died at the Chichester Hospital after a stroke, so we were also looking for a house with an annexe to accommodate his father, Ewart, who would otherwise have been alone. Poplars had that too, a ground-floor flat in the converted stables.

We set about buying Poplars Farm House immediately. It was not an easy task as we had to sell Ewart's cottage in the New Forest, and Patrick's house in Kent simultaneously, but eventually with the help of the understanding vendors, the Carpenters, we were able to achieve it and within two months we moved in.

My only sadness was that my beloved Blue never lived to see it: he died aged ten of a heart attack two weeks before we moved. The lifespan of dobermanns is seldom long. Blue had not been well for a few days, often waking me up in the middle of the night, which was unusual for him. The local vet diagnosed gastroenteritis, entirely wrongly; had he got it right, I'm sure heart pills could have kept Blue going considerably longer. Joan Bakewell and her husband Jack Emery were with me at the time he collapsed in the street, and they rang the vet. A whole hour passed and he didn't show up, by which time Blue was dead. People were so kind – a little girl put her coat over him in case he was cold and a passing lady motorist helped us load him into the car to drive him to the vet's. There they took the body and they presented me, crying as I was, indifferently with a bill for twenty-five pounds. I never returned to that veterinary practice again.

We missed Blue terribly, constantly listening for his tread that would never come, and decided to get another dobermann. There is something about having owned a dobermann that makes you unable to contemplate another breed. We realized too that Poplars Farm House was far more isolated and vulnerable than anywhere either of us had lived before, and a dobermann would be our biggest asset in the local war against burglars, as only a lunatic would take on a dobermann defending its own territory. Blue was loyal and loving, and for ten years had been my constant protector. I found it painful to be without him.

I rang the Kennel Club who gave me the number of the Dobermann Club. We had decided on a brown dobermann bitch so there wouldn't be comparisons with Blue, a black male.

'I would like a red' – red being the correct term for brown – 'bitch who is wonderful with children,' I said. In my experience such dogs are natural guard dogs and the softer their character, the better. I was dispatched to Great Missenden and sure enough, there, on the floor, was a one-year-old child with three dobermann bitches and one dobermann male, all equally soppy animals. I was taken to see twelve tiny puppies and, unable to choose between them, decided on the one who managed to untie my shoe laces.

It is amazing how all the attention a new puppy needs can quickly dry your tears over the death of the old. In a way I feel it is rather a compliment to the old dog – they leave such a vacuum in your life that you attempt to fill it.

The choice of a name for the little puppy was a matter of disagreement. I wanted to call her Scarlet or Eliza, Patrick didn't care for Scarlet and thought Eliza would remind him of the time he directed *My Fair Lady* with

Rex Harrison which, in its New York run, had proved a less than serene experience. Patrick wanted to call her Sophie, because it had an old-fashioned ring, a name which I didn't particularly like for a dog, but in the end I conceded the point. So Sophie she was. Now I come to think of it I've conceded on most of the other animals' names as well, but then there are rather a lot of animals!

Sophie proved enchanting – the most intelligent and obedient of dogs – and she never put a foot wrong. It was through Sophie that I learnt which of Blue's characteristics had been his own, and which were those of the dobermann breed. Sophie resembled Blue in many ways, being clever, very good-natured and easy to train, although in the country there wasn't the need for the rigid traffic discipline Blue had been subjected to. However, as with Blue, intimidated by the dobermann reputation, people often misread her intentions. Blue's favourite way of greeting friends was to clamp his mouth around their wrist and tug them indoors, Sophie's way of saying 'Hello' was even more frightening. She would give the most enormous grin, but as this meant curling back her upper lip and revealing her huge canine teeth, people would retreat down the drive as fast as they could. But when you knew that it was only a smile and not a snarl it was the most lovely welcome to come home to. One day I found a local delivery man putting a package down right in front of her. 'Aren't you afraid?' I asked in amazement.

'Oh, no. Jock the postman's told me she's harmless,' he said.

Next time I saw Jock I had a quiet word with him: 'You must stop telling people how nice Sophie is. You're ruining her reputation!'

'Aye, I s'pose you're right,' he replied. 'It wouldn't do for the burglars to know your ferocious-looking dog was simply smiling at them!'

Soon after we had installed Sophie we learnt of a white golden retriever puppy, Ben, that needed a home. When he was six months old his owner had a baby and decided she didn't want the dog any more. With such a large garden for them to play in it was easy to be a two-dog family and Patrick readily agreed to take him on. At least now when we were both working and had to leave the house Sophie would have company. Ben proved to be a big asset to the household; he adored Sophie and in their puppyhood it was useful to have the two together as the bundles of energy wore each other out. They would play for hours and then collapse on their beanbags motionless while peace reigned once more.

Ben had just one problem as a puppy. He would be so excited to see you in the morning that he could not stop himself from peeing on the spot. As a result every morning we would race through the kitchen into the garden so he could vent his delight out there!

The location of Poplars Farm House was ideal. Apart from the closeness to the theatre, we were only a short drive from East Head, the most glorious long, sandy spit of beach where Sophie and Ben could splash in the surf, swim and retrieve logs to their hearts' content. Behind the house a footpath wound for miles through farmland and there Sophie and Ben discovered for the first time the joys of chasing rabbits and hares, and pheasants and partridges which would take off suddenly right under their noses. Once, Patrick, on a morning walk, watched while Sophie sported with a mysterious bushy-tailed red dog – only to discover it was a young fox. The encounter only lasted a moment. The two dogs never caught a thing – not even the things, like rats, that we would have liked them to catch.

4

The Kamikaze Cat and the Showbiz Donkey

Our main problem at Poplars was that within two weeks of the Carpenters' moving out with their cat, Timothy, the mice had moved in. They were everywhere: in the lofts, in the larder, under the sinks, in the cupboards, in all the rooms, in the garage and in the barn. They would scuttle above our ceiling as we tried to sleep, and we even had them swinging on the curtains behind us as we watched television. Something had to be done. First we tried a humane mousetrap but no matter how enticing the food we put in it as bait they ignored it; eventually we resorted to a fierce metal trap, but the mice managed expertly to remove the cheese without getting caught. Meanwhile there was a mouse population explosion going on.

Even worse, one day Patrick's father, who had by now moved in with us, announced there were 'ratis' on his bird table. I expected some form of wild bird not previously known to me along with the redwings and fieldfares, but to my horror I was shortly enlightened by the appearance of three large brown rats climbing the stand and munching the birdseed just in front of his french windows. What could we do? Finally Patrick decided, on his own initiative, that a cat was the only answer. Word had already reached us of the redoubtable Min Flower from Cat Rescue and, in desperation, I rang her up.

'We have something of a problem,' I explained. 'We moved into Poplars Farm House a month ago and we're infested with mice and rats. To compound the situation we have a dobermann bitch and a retriever who have loved chasing cats all their lives. What can we do?'

'A cat will usually get the better of a dog,' said Min, 'but you don't want a timid one, and you won't want a tiny kitten. Why don't you come over, there's always at least thirty rescued cats here, and we'll see if there's one that will suit you.'

A visit to Min Flower's for an animal lover was a miraculous experience. First to greet you behind the big gate were not dogs, but two remarkable pet goats, then you noticed a profusion of wild birds amidst cats of various sizes and breeds and, unusually, more than two hundred guinea-pigs cropping the grass of her large lawn.

'Don't the cats eat the birds and the guinea-pigs?' I asked.

'For some reason they don't,' said Min. 'They all live together in perfect harmony. You've met the goats, but don't be alarmed when they wander into the house with you, they're perfectly house-trained and live inside with us.'

Indeed they were, but it was a bit disconcerting when you found a goat sitting on the sofa next to you.

Inside the sitting room there were kittens, and Min's own cats, which were mainly Devon and Cornish Rexes. Enchanting, sweet-natured, crinkle-coated creatures, because they look so different with their corduroy fur, they are more difficult to find homes for. Min had just rescued seventeen from a flat where they had been found a week after their elderly owner died, and they were in a sorry state. Kittens ranged about everywhere, and on the subject of procreation Min was quietly determined.

'If I give you a young cat, you will have to sign a contract saying you will have it neutered.'

'If it's a lovely cat isn't that rather a shame?' said I naively.

'Shame?' Min almost choked. 'There are a *thousand* cats put to sleep every day. Shame!' she repeated angrily. 'I don't want people who have cats from me contributing to that number.' I absolutely saw her point – it was heart-rending to see how many unwanted kittens, waifs and strays, ended up on her doorstep.

'The one I think will suit you is a little black half-Burmese chap of about four months. He's full of beans, very quick and very resilient.' She was right, he was the obvious choice; a lot of the kittens were soft and cuddly, but we didn't want a cat that would just want to sit on your knee all day – there was work to be done. I thanked Min Flower profusely, signed the agreement, gave the charity a voluntary contribution, and took my small wriggly purring bundle home.

Sophie was aggrieved. Did we really expect her to live with a cat? Kim, as Patrick christened him, after Kipling's artful hero, was oblivious to the hostility around him, and seemed to find keeping one step ahead of Sophie rather a game. Within two weeks of his arrival Sophie had decided she couldn't accept him but could safely ignore him, and looked the other way whenever Kim entered the room. Ben, in true retriever style, paid no attention to his arrival whatsoever.

It was remarkable how accurate was Min's character reading of such a young cat – he was totally fearless and soon became known as Kim the Kamikaze Cat. Although tiny, Kim despatched mice with great alacrity although he had trouble with the rats which were considerably larger than he was. However, in this, with great resourcefulness, he enlisted Sophie as an ally. He would drive the rats towards her, and she in turn would toss them in the air and break their necks, creating a most successful partnership. When not too busy hunting

Kim would come and hold lengthy conversations with you (doubtless the result of his Burmese genes), wind himself around your legs and climb up your back to the top of your head where he would proceed to clean your hair, as though seeking imaginary lice!

The curtains stopped waving, silence prevailed above the ceiling, the birds returned to the bird table, and Kim became a welcome addition to the family. In the absence of other cats to amuse him he would come on daily six-mile walks with the two dogs without a moment's trepidation, often getting sidetracked by a vole on the way. When he had lagged behind too much he would suddenly do a mad sprint, clearing ditches with huge kangaroo-type leaps until he caught up with us once again.

Sophie and Ben came to think of him as some form of Yorkshire terrier and no longer objected to his presence. In their eyes he wasn't a cat at all, he had earned the status of Honorary Dog.

Following our move into Poplars Farm House, and a stressful theatrical season, we were both exhausted and decided that we were in need of a holiday. But where to go in October? The summer we had hardly noticed was already on the wane. Then Derek Nimmo rang up and asked Patrick if he would like to direct *The Secretary Bird* on a tour of the Far East. It was not something Patrick had anticipated doing – but it would mean an all-expenses-paid holiday for both of us. We decided that Patrick would direct the play in Hong Kong, and then we'd be free to go on to Thailand, Bali, Singapore or Malaysia, depending on the weather, for a rest.

The weather was the problem – Hong Kong was literally a wash-out; the monsoons had arrived a month early and you were either drenched or sweltered in your raincoat. Bali and Thailand were apparently equally sodden, so we followed Derek's suggestion and went to the 'Paradise Island' of Tioman, off the Malaysian coast. It *was* beautiful, but our stay there was not without hitches and discomfort, not to mention flies and mosquitoes. We were not sorry to leave, and, back at Poplars Farm House I wondered why we had ever bothered to go away, with such a paradise at home. The dogs were thrilled to see us again, and Kim twined himself around my legs, purring away. They seemed more pleased to see us than Ewart was – he had been so spoiled by Gladys King, a kind, motherly woman who had come in to help, that I suspect he saw our return as an end to all her cossetting.

Some three weeks after our return, as Patrick was preparing the new season in Chichester, I was having tea with an actor friend, Richard Freeman, at our flat in London. Suddenly I began to vibrate all over, and a strange heat, which seemed to start in my lower back, began to work its way upwards. I tried lying down, but that didn't seem to help, and I had an irrational fear that if that intense heat reached my head I would die. Richard managed to get hold of my doctor who came swiftly to the flat. 'Have you been anywhere strange?' he asked. I told him the Far East, whereupon he gave me a prescription for antibiotics – quite the wrong thing, it seems, but I recovered sufficiently to keep going, and by adopting a Chinese macrobiotic diet recommended by another actor friend, Keith Michell, I managed to keep the sickness at bay and, although very thin and extremely weak, I returned to normal life in Chichester.

As Patrick continued to plan the coming season, I sat back and took stock. The inside of the house was more-or-less finished; now for the first time I was able to turn my attention to the grounds which consisted of four acres of land, half an acre of it cultivated.

The Carpenters had filled the herbaceous borders with delicate, scented, tobacco plants, which were fine for their shi-tzu, but our dogs had decimated them instantly. What was needed was plants with spikes and thorns – roses, and other such dobermann and retriever-proof shrubs.

The remainder of the three and a half acres consisted of two rectangular paddocks, both rather overgrown, and dock-infested. Hidden away inside the traditional Sussex barn I had stumbled across a rusting Allen scythe, like a huge lawn-mower, which had obviously been used to keep down the paddock. How boring, I thought, a gentle grass-eating animal would be far more rewarding. It was while I was still pondering that point that an advertisement in the *West Sussex Gazette* caught my eye: 'Wanted. Home for show-biz donkey, box, shoe, cart £300'. I was intrigued. The going rate for a donkey was £50, so what could be so special about this one? I rang the Eastbourne telephone number quoted in the newspaper.

'I'm ringing about your donkey . . . could you possibly tell me why it's so expensive?'

'It includes the cart. The donkey Henry is only £100,' said the owner. It still seemed a little excessive.

'But the normal price for a donkey is £50,' I haggled.

'Ah, but Henry is no ordinary donkey. He's a star, there's nothing he won't do, and all the children adore him.'

'I'll give it some thought and get back to you,' I said. I was still feeling under par and was a bit apprehensive. Would I be able to cope with something as big as a donkey? That night my sleep was interrupted by worries: did donkeys need hay or straw? Would I find a farrier in the area? Would local friends help out if I were working? Would the neighbours complain if he brayed too loudly?

Was our fencing sufficient to keep him in? My doubts increased. In the morning I picked up the telephone.

'Mr Smith, I'm not feeling too brilliant at the moment, so I'm afraid I won't be able to come to Eastbourne to see Henry.'

'No problem,' said Peter Smith. 'I'll bring him to you.'

'But supposing I don't take to him?' I replied, my resolve failing.

'Don't worry, missis, you don't have to have him if you don't like him.'

Something in the tone of his voice told me we would like him.

The next day a small horse-box was driven up the drive of Poplars, and Henry stepped out. He was, it must be said, very beautiful as donkeys go, pure grey with a dark cross on his shoulders and a little white star on his forehead. Mr Smith had left nothing to chance, and came equipped for the audition with a ten-year-old girl to put Henry through his paces. He walked, he trotted, he turned, he cantered in perfect delicate-hoofed dressage-style. He was certainly the ideal donkey. All doubts were dispelled, whether I was ill or not, Henry obviously had to stay. Besides, ours had been the only enquiry, and without us Henry faced an uncertain future. Even no future at all. The one hundred pounds was paid over including saddle, halter, and tack, and Henry moved in.

Then the nightmare began: 'Hee-haw, hee-haw, hee-haw' throughout the night, and through the day. We learnt quickly an elementary lesson – that you cannot have *one* donkey, you have to have two. Sid and Cathy Green the elderly couple next door, who have their bedroom overlooking the paddock, were getting fractious: 'That moke's lonely,' said Sid, 'and he's keeping Cathy awake at night. What do you intend to do about it?' With the circles under our eyes getting darker too, and most of the locals looking bleary-eyed, even Patrick was inclined to agree that what was needed was another donkey to keep Henry company. Anything to stop the nocturnal cacophony.

My mother, upon hearing of our plight, offered to resolve the situation. 'I'll buy you a female donkey for Christmas,' she told me. This time there were no advertisements in the local papers, so I tracked down our local donkey man and farrier, Peter Lingfield, who, I knew, had a whole field full of donkeys next to the Chichester by-pass. A picturesque and pastoral sight.

'Could I possibly buy a donkey from you?' I asked him. 'Ours needs a companion.'

'Just go along and pick one from the field,' he said, 'but not the white donkey, that's the jack; the rest are geldings or jennies. One of them'll cost you £50.'

Off I went to the road-side paddock and gazed across at the forty donkeys, rather at a loss as to which to pick. At that moment a little girl wandered by, and some donkeys trotted over to see her. Their curiosity was beguiling.

'Do you know them?' I asked.

'Oh yes,' she replied, 'and sometimes I'm allowed to ride them.'

'Perhaps you could advise me then. You see we have a lonely boy-donkey at home, and we want to buy him a jenny for company. I'd like one that children can ride as well.' Without a moment's hesitation she pointed to a very pretty brown and white donkey and said: 'She's the best, the friendliest, I ride her all the time.'

'Does she have a name?' I asked.

'None of them have names,' she answered. 'Shame, isn't it?'

The little brown and white ass was delivered after dark on Christmas Eve, and the following morning, gazing out of our bedroom window Patrick couldn't believe his eyes.

'Is it my imagination or do I see *two* donkeys out there?'

'You probably had a bit too much to drink last night,' I suggested.

'I should have known something was up,' he said. 'I slept like a log.'

We were almost as enchanted with the new arrival as Henry, who, unable to believe his luck, had become totally speechless and could only stare at her with a mixture of adoration and awe. The jenny, however, simply kicked and bit him whenever he came near, thereby establishing that she had the upper hand in their future relationship together. 'Not unlike the human condition' was my husband's comment.

The next problem was what to call her: 'Henry and . . .'. To us the answer was obvious. Our next-door neighbours at our previous house in Kent were called Henry and Frances Susskind. They had once raised an orphan ewe called Floppy, that used to delight in coming for country walks with us, Blue, and their Afghan, Babu. When Floppy was fully grown, in an attempt to make her more of a sheep and less of a dog, a tiny ram called Jenkin was brought in. However, she seemed to ignore him, particularly as she was by now so large that he would have needed a ladder to mount her. Jenkin was returned in disgrace to the farmer, but proved a much maligned ram as Floppy later produced two adorable little lambs which our friends had christened in our honour 'Patrick and Alexandra'.

With one donkey already called Henry, what better therefore than to name the other after Frances? So 'Henry and Frances' they became, the Susskinds didn't object, and everything progressed peacefully. Apart from one strange phenomenon: Frances seemed to be growing fatter, and fatter, and fatter. Was it our imagination? Was Frances over-feeding?

I tried to lay my hands on as many donkey textbooks as I could, but there seemed to be a dearth of them. I came across endless books about ponies and horses, but nowhere could I find one which would tell me how much hay to give a donkey, how much bran mash, how many pony nuts, how much sugar beet ... In fact, I could glean hardly any information at all about how to look after a donkey, and meanwhile Frances kept on growing. Finally we called in Mr Vinnicombe, our ever-tolerant veterinarian, and he gave his diagnosis: 'She's pregnant.'

'But she can't be!' I exclaimed.

Patrick was convinced that I had picked a pregnant donkey on purpose. I hadn't, but, thinking back I realized that as a female comes into season every three weeks, and there had been the white jack donkey in Mr Lingfield's field, it was possible that all the jennies were pregnant. It certainly wasn't our Henry's doing. He, poor old chap, had been castrated long ago.

'How pregnant is she?' I asked.

'Difficult to say,' Mr Vinnicombe replied. 'The pregnancy lasts twelve months.'

We became anxious prospective foster parents, but could not stay chained to the house without a definite date fixed for the birth. In the event, it was our dog-walking friend Diana Carver who had the good fortune to witness it, when she was staying at the farmhouse in April. We were attending Shakespeare's birthday celebrations at Stratford. Frances evidently coped perfectly and discreetly gave birth to a tiny white jenny donkey with small brown spots. Henry, however, perhaps enraged that it wasn't grey, like him, became jealous and tried to kill it. Diana forcibly removed him to the other paddock and put mother and baby in the warm straw-filled stable we had prepared for that moment. We arrived back from Stratford that evening to the glorious spectacle of a slim Frances suckling her adorable white baby with its huge furry ears, great big brown eyes, and tiny fragile legs. When donkeys are born their ears lie flat against their heads like a spaniel's, but regrettably by the time we arrived her ears were already up. We resolved then and there to call the foal Phoebe, after the rustic character in Shakespeare's *As You Like It*, which Patrick was directing at the time.

Finally all went well, Henry grudgingly accepted the little foal, and the three grazed in quiet harmony in our two small paddocks. It was a heavenly sight, and attracted many a passer-by.

Phoebe's birth was not the only one that spring. As adolescence approached, Sophie had driven us demented with her 'nesting' which usually meant digging up the Wilton carpet. We therefore decided to let her have a litter before being spayed, while we still had some carpet left. On reflection this was ill-advised, as there are so many large unwanted guard dogs available at Rescue Centres. But, knowing nothing of that at the time, we took Sophie off to see a gorgeous black and tan dobermann, called Dante, who was a Cruft's contender. It was a true love-match. They took to each other immediately, and we returned home to await the happy event. We did everything according to the book and Jim King, Gladys's husband, was called in to construct a large whelping box so Sophie wouldn't crush the puppies when they were born. With her father having sired a record seventeen puppies in one litter and her mother thirteen we were expecting a somewhat similar number from Sophie. As the weeks progressed we fed Sophie on the best cuts of meat, fresh vegetables and vitamins, and homoeopathic remedies for pregnant bitches to give her numerous brood the best start in life. But when the time came, nothing happened. Finally, in desperation, we called in Mr Vinnicombe, the vet. He gave her an injection to induce the birth and Sophie in an agitated state disappeared under rubble in the barn. There we could just make out the form of a tiny black puppy. According to the book, for safety's sake, she had to have her puppies in the whelping box, so a rescue had to be mounted and the little thing was brought in. Sophie's response to that was to pick the puppy up in her mouth directly, and take it back to the barn. Alarmingly there continued to be no sign of any more puppies, so once more Mr Vinnicombe was called in to advise. However, just before he came two tiny black legs appeared, and we knew from our reading that this was an emergency; unless the puppy was pulled out quickly, it would suffocate. Amongst the barn debris we pulled out the little mite. To my dismay, it wasn't breathing.

Give it a drop of brandy, said the book: one, two, three, four drops, finally the alcoholic shock got it going, and by the time Mr Vinnicombe arrived all was well. Sophie had an expression of gratitude and surprise on her face.

'If no more puppies emerge, we'll have to take her in,' said Mr Vinnicombe. 'There may be some serious trouble, and an X-ray will show us what's going on.' No further offspring appeared, and he and I took poor anxious Sophie to the surgery, while Patrick and Gladys King stayed to mind the two puppies at home. I waited outside the surgery.

The vet emerged from the room. 'That's it, I'm afraid – there aren't any more.' I looked at him incredulously – all that steak and that expensive hand-made whelping box for just two minuscule puppies.

'Look at the X-ray – there aren't any tiny skeletons, she's completely clear.'

I drove home, stunned – thirteen or seventeen was the expected number and all we had was two. When we arrived home Sophie went straight to the whelping box, removed her two puppies and this time took them to her bean bag where she was in such imminent danger of squashing them that for the first week either the loyal Gladys or I slept near them on a mattress every night.

As time progressed it became evident that having only two puppies was a blessing in disguise. First, because we wouldn't have to resort to selling them to total strangers, and second, because the noise level, which was bad enough with two, would obviously have been a great deal worse with thirteen. Our insurance broker friend Jim Fresson had asked for a brown bitch, but in the event was happy to settle for a black male. We had also planned on keeping one of Sophie's brown daughters, but there was only another black male.

'You can't keep a male dobermann with another male and a bitch, even if it is the mother. There will be trouble,' warned the Dobermann Club. We thought we knew better. Legs (Patrick later changed his name to Kipling, when he worked on a show about the writer, with Alex McCowan) was so extremely timid and sensitive that we could never have imagined that he would ever change. He had the sweetest disposition.

Mating Sophie with Dante was technically called an outcross, a process often frowned upon by the breeders who wish to perpetuate certain traits and genes. I simply wanted healthy puppies and thought this would be more likely if there had been no in-breeding at all.

Sophie came from the American line where they encourage the ears to stand up and Dante was from the English line where the ears are trained to stay down. As a result both of Sophie's puppies not only had lop-sided grins, but lop-sided ears as well; not exactly Cruft's winners, but very handsome and extremely strong and healthy dogs.

Sophie and Kipling together had a far greater range of vocal acrobatics than Blue had ever had. From an early stage, they orchestrated their howls and wails.

Each morning began at eight sharp, with a perfectly harmonized yodelling duet with Sophie as soprano and Kipling just beneath her as tenor. This concert would persist for a full five minutes, if necessary with encores, until they had succeeded in waking up their sleepy owners. Once downstairs there were passionate snorts of greeting before they positioned themselves side by side by the back door to await their breakfast. This was speedily demolished, and a daily assault was then made, to test the carefully closed door that separated them from the cat food. Their attention then switched to Patrick, who after a sequence of determined whines conceded defeat and took them for their two-field morning walk. This was along a series of local ripes (Sussex ditches) and beside our back field of eleven acres, called Poplars Eleven. Mother and son often hunted as a pair, giving sharp, high screeches of excitement as they sought out and pursued their quarry and sometimes, unfortunately, even succeeded in cutting it off. Normally obedient, once on the scent they became deaf to all our frantic cries.

The rest of the day would proceed calmly enough only interspersed with barks at strangers and what we called the 'Hounds of the Baskervilles' routine for recognizable car engines of friends drawing up outside. This was another extended ululating routine mainly in B flat, giving the illusion of someone being savaged by Siberian wolves.

The afternoon walk followed the same procedure as the morning one, only with the attention turned to me as chief afternoon dog walker. Signs such as the front door being locked (we walk out the back), the answering machine being switched on, wellies, coats or hats appearing, were all accompanied by sniffs of pleasure. Their dinner time followed shortly afterwards, with the same two book-ends stationed outside the back door. During our supper our badly trained dogs offered their paws all too frequently and Sophie, more determined than Kipling, would even do a 'dead dog' routine, rolling over winningly on her back, until her request was met.

In fact Sophie's major flaw was her obsessive love of food. She had been known to eat eight unattended duck eggs, butter, margarine, pâté and garlic bread at one go. She particularly liked parties, preferably with young children and circulated constantly around the guests, nudging their elbows so that they would drop the contents of their plates on the floor where she would then proceed to eat them. One Christmas party was almost a disaster; just as I was about to usher the guests into the dining room for a buffet supper I noticed the Yule log had changed shape. She hadn't eaten it, she had merely rearranged the icing. Secure in the knowledge that the dogs had been de-wormed the previous weekend I simply pushed the now slightly thinner icing back in place.

In the course of a rather grand dinner party which was attended by the Duke and Duchess of Richmond and Gordon, Lord and Lady Norwich, and several distinguished Cathedral clergy, the following drama occurred backstage. After the main course, as I left the dining room carrying a stack of plates, I stepped on a dead rat in the hall. Kim, the cat, had brought it in as a present. I proceeded to the kitchen, and there I found two large saucepans both upside-down on the floor. Of the original contents, four leftover pheasant carcasses, there was no sign – nor was there of Sophie who, anticipating a ticking off, was hiding away in the garden. Poor Kipling, drooling at the mouth, had obviously not been allowed one single bite. Sophie had eaten the lot, bones and giblets and all. The dinner party, may I say, continued with our eminent guests sipping their coffee unaware.

5

Clever Koi and Paddock Pandemonium

From time to time I would also act in one of the Chichester plays, but every time I did, I felt exhausted, and I remained very thin, still suffering from tummy troubles. Finally, Leslie Evershed-Martin, the founder of the theatre, suggested I visit the Tropical Diseases Hospital in London. I had by now seen about twelve doctors and specialists in Chichester, Brighton and London all to no avail. Dr Bryceson the expert in foreign parasitical diseases gave me some tablets and cured me immediately. He warned that it would take a while to recover fully, but I was in for a marvellous tonic. The telephone went: it was my Canadian agent asking me if I would like to star opposite Kirk Douglas and James Coburn in a Western called *Draw*. Would I not! It was the zenith of my film career.

It is rare for an English actress to be asked to star in an American cowboy feature, but in this case the part I was playing was that of a Shakespearian thespian (so a British accent was desirable) who was on tour with a troupe of actors. I was then not only kidnapped by Kirk Douglas, but rescued by James Coburn – oh, that it could happen in every movie!

Kirk Douglas, apart from being the highly professional producer of the film, was also very generous to work with, staying around for close-ups, and giving the off-lines

and generally being most considerate. As I was still suffering the after-effects of the digestive illness when we went
out to restaurants he even went so far as ordering brown
rice from the hotel, in order that I could take it with me.
He was most kind. James Coburn whose fan I had been
since *Our Man Flint* was much more reclusive, staying in
his winnebago a lot, but I believe he had health problems
of his own as he was suffering from a severe form of
arthritis. The fascination of the film though was the
Calgary Cowboys who really gave meaning to the expression 'live it up' when they gave their lively parties. Each
one had a rank, almost like in the army, which was
revealed by their belt buckles, their stetsons, their boots,
from which you could tell what status they held in the
Calgary Stampede. It was an education just being around
them. Their horses too were magnificent, huge beasts.
One, called Babe, was specially trained to get the wagon
started, to do which she would rear up on command and
crash down, getting it moving by her weight. Kirk
Douglas's horse was a handsome beige and white stallion;
but halfway through the day one of its several doubles
would be called in when it became too exhausted. The
only trouble was that no two horses were the same, so the
make-up department was kept very busy painting them. It
was almost as complicated as a Spanish film I made when
they tried to make cows look like yaks by putting white
fur coats on them!

However, all too soon my favourite film was over and
it was away from Canada, Kirk and cowboys, and back
to the Chichester Theatre and my animals.

With the dollars I had earned on *Draw* I decided to fulfil
one of my ambitions – to create a pond of large koi carp.
Since the days of my keeping shubunkins, golden orf,
blackamoors and fantails in tanks in my London flat I

had always loved koi. However, I had had no success
with them – they hated tanks and would throw
themselves out on to the floor.

Maybe it's because I'm a Piscean that I am so fascinated by fish, particularly by the koi which cannot be
matched for intelligence or iridescent beauty. In a large
pond they can attain a great size and age and can seem
positively human.

Do fish think and feel? According to my friend Mark
Luffman, a fish expert, they do, and I tend to subscribe
to the same theory. Recently when a beautiful large black
and white fish was ill with gill flukes and gasping for air
on the surface the other fish took it in turns to swim
underneath and support it all day. Can this have been
mere coincidence? They are also territorial and assume
the same position to sleep in at night (you can check this
by shining a torch into the water). Other koi owners tell
tales of ringing bells at feed time and the fish assembling
accordingly. Our fish recognize and swim towards us
whenever they catch sight of us while they vanish at the
appearance of strangers, another peculiar phenomenon.
Mark has a warmwater catfish in his 'Fish House' (which
takes up half his garden) and people are amazed at the
relationship he has with it; it goes berserk whenever he
enters the room and if he puts his hand in the tank it
rubs against him and caresses him for several minutes at
a time. A friend of his recently introduced a mirror carp
into his pond full of koi. The mirror carp was used to
being fed on 'boilies', which is a food they are particularly partial to, but other fish are not, and which sink to
the bottom of the water. For a week the koi were fed
their usual pellets on the surface and the mirror carp
dived down for his boilies; however by the end of the
seven days the carp had taken stock of the fact that there
was no competition for his food, and the koi were being

given something else on the surface. The result was that thereafter the carp ate all the koi food first and then dived down for his own. Who said fish weren't intelligent?

A reasonable age for koi is seventy but the record is held by a female koi in Japan who is 226 years old, weighs 20 pounds and is two and a half feet long. As a side benefit the larger they grow the more valuable they become. It is ironic that a donkey is worth about £50 and koi carp twelve inches long about £200 to £2000. People are known to have alarm systems guarding their koi, we only have two dobermann pinschers!

The only unaesthetic touch is the net with which we unfortunately have to cover the pond to protect the fish from herons and other predators. Some people use fake herons and others have a wire round their fish pond, but both methods are ineffectual compared with a basic net. I support the heron community stationed at the Brent Lodge Bird Hospital a few fields away, but I am not pleased to see them when they sit in the meadow behind us, waiting for the dogs to go for their walk and leave the pond unattended. If a heron can wade into a pond his feet will emit an enticing odour which attracts the fish to him so that he can pick them off one by one. The object therefore is to prevent him at all costs getting into it. Kim, the cat, had also quickly become an expert fisherman, so the net solved a dual purpose, and kept him out of it as well.

As Kim grew older, although still diminutive, he grew too big for his boots and we were rather upset when, having exhausted the rodent population, he turned his attention to moorhens, partridges, rabbits and pheasants; nothing seemed too large for tiny Kim's appetite. When Sophie had her puppies even they were potential victims and she had to guard them from him night and day. Once they had grown large enough to stand up to him he would play with them for hours on end and it must have been a funny sight to see us out walking with Ben, the retriever, Sophie, her two puppies, and Kim.

Finally, however, the worst happened and one terrible day Kim failed to return home. We walked for miles calling as we went, for days, weeks, and months; even Sophie and Ben understood and tried to sniff him out without success. We put advertisements in the local shop window and newspapers, broadcast on local radio, and followed up every lead, but none proved to be little black Kim with two white hairs on his chest and a kink, like a cartoon cat, in his tail. The odds were that he had been run over by one of the lunatics who regularly drive at eighty miles an hour down our narrow country lane or, less likely, that with his Napoleon complex he had had a confrontation with the local fox. Having a pet just disappear has to be the worst form of torture and for months we hoped and feared; even now, years later, I find I look intently at every black cat in the area, hoping against hope to recognize little Kim.

After two months the mice and rats had taken stock of Kim's disappearance and moved back in force and, while we still hoped he would return, a substitute had to be found. Once again Min was consulted.

'I suggest you get two this time,' she said, 'as they are less likely to roam so far afield – but, most important, you must get them on the same day. That way each will think the other already lives there and not assert territorial ownership.'

Fate was shortly to play a hand when, on a visit to my mother in Hove I popped into the local pet shop for some dog food. An old lady wandered in clutching a beautiful white cat.

'Excuse me,' she said, 'I've been looking after this stray, but I have to go into hospital – can you take it?'

She was addressing the shop's owners, but before they could reply I found myself speaking: 'I'll take it – you see, I don't have my cat any more.'

Obviously relieved, the lady thrust her wnite charge into my arms and swiftly left the shop. The owners said they couldn't have taken it anyway, so my arrival had been opportune, to say the least.

By a happy coincidence, as we arrived home a neighbour turned up on the doorstep with a minute black kitten: 'We heard you lost your little black cat and wondered if you would like this one; it was found in the road in Chichester.' Min's theory of the simultaneous arrival worked a treat and Blackie and Whitey (*not* named by Patrick) took to each other immediately. Whitey belied his effete snowy beauty and was courageous beyond belief, attacking rats, weasels, stoats, wild cats and even dogs, and became his little black friend's protector. Like Kim, they came on long walks with Sophie, Kipling and Ben. During the course of one promenade Kipling put up a pheasant and went after it, scaring Blackie in the process. Whitey went into immediate dervish-like action and hurled himself through the air to land on poor Ben's back, having assumed that he was the culprit. While he spat and hissed we unhooked his claws from an astonished Ben's body. Fortunately a retriever has so much hair that there was no discernible damage, but all the dogs took note, and for a few days gave Whitey a very wide berth.

Whitey was not very human-orientated, maybe because of his vagrant years, but his great redeeming feature was his affection for little Blackie and every night they would curl up together in a chair with Whitey's paws wrapped round the little black cat.

As the months passed and Blackie and Whitey settled in, I had to accept that it was unlikely that Kim would ever return, though I still watched out for his noble Burmese face and twisty tail.

At the same time as our cat numbers were growing, the donkey population was also on the increase. The birth of Phoebe had received a lot of publicity in the local newspaper. Henry, Frances and the little foal were now grazing harmoniously in our two small paddocks, but all that was to change.

The telephone rang. It is odd how a simple telephone call can often bring discord to an otherwise tranquil world.

'It's the switchboard at the Chichester Festival Theatre here. We've just had a phone call from an elderly couple at Pagham who want you to take over their donkey. They've left their telephone number.'

I rang the number: 'I'm sorry, but we really don't want any more donkeys. You see, we don't have enough pasture.'

'Oh,' said the elderly lady, 'you seem so kind to donkeys and we need a good, safe home for Chérie or Blossom, as she's called. We're too old now to take her for walks and the only place we could put her would be in a field at Pagham Harbour where louts have been known to slash the ponies with knives.'

'Well, that doesn't sound like a good idea at all,' I said, 'but surely there must be somewhere else. Would you like the telephone number of Sidmouth Donkey Rescue?'

She ignored the suggestion and went on: 'You see your house looks out over the paddocks so she'd be safe, and she's such a special donkey; she lived with a labrador all her life and thinks she's a dog. She even gives you her hoof for Polo mints, and brings her bowl to you in her mouth for more food when she's finished.'

I was a little intrigued, I must admit, and relayed the

strange tale to Patrick. Reluctantly, but curious, he agreed to see this Chérie or Blossom.

When we arrived at the address in a residential street we were appalled. The donkey was kept in a tiny shed in a garden twelve foot square, sheer cruelty for an animal of that size. Fed a diet of sticky buns, white bread, and hay, the poor beast was expected to forage for grass on her daily walk round the kerb-sides of Pagham, and the old couple were getting too frail to take her any more. Chérie was put through her party tricks for us, which were impressive, but they played no part in our mutual conclusion: the donkey had to be removed from such irresponsible, albeit well meaning, owners.

We couldn't stand her names so she quickly became Cherry Blossom, and a horse-box was sent to get her. After twenty sticky buns were proffered she finally climbed in and was whisked away to Poplars Farm House. But once she was there, mayhem ensued. The happy family of Henry, Frances, and Phoebe hated the newcomer on sight and Cherry Blossom, who thought she was a dog, would have nothing to do with them at all.

'Hee-haw, hee-haw.' They screamed mutual loathing at each other all day long – and all night.

'Are you going to find another home for that moke?' said Sid Green rather edgily. 'Cathy's not getting any sleep again.' After a week of this paddock pandemonium I started to ask around, and Mr Bridger, the farmer, would have taken her for his young son Joe, but reneged when I explained if he wanted a quiet life he really needed two. However, just as we and Sid reached our wits' end, suddenly, after three weeks, the noise abated. Cherry Blossom had come on heat, had fallen in love with Henry, and had decided to be a donkey after all.

During her years of incarceration in a tiny garden

Cherry Blossom had perfected the art of escaping with Houdini-like expertise. There was no bolt, lock, or chain, that she could not dismantle, and her answer to the wooden stakes and barbed wire which formed our hitherto adequate, but fragile fencing, was to chew away at the base of each rustic pole until it fell over, at which point she, followed by the others, would step out and go for a walk down the lane.

'If those mokes get in with my bees there's going to be hell to pay,' said Sid Green. And, even though his shotgun was stashed away, I knew this was not a threat to be taken lightly.

'It won't happen again,' I said meekly, desperately hoping it wouldn't, but afraid that it might.

Jim King, our handyman, came to the rescue and stoutly replaced each wooden pole with a metal one interlaced with endless reels of barbed wire muttering, 'Cherry Blossom, you cow,' as she tried to prevent him. The gates remained a problem until we tried combination-lock bicycle chains – these out-foxed even her.

We used to gaze out serenely across our rustic paddocks. Alas, no more. Since the arrival of Cherry Blossom the Escapologist, we look out over metal fortifications which rival Wormwood Scrubs. Only the watch-towers are missing. However, at least we managed, on the whole, to keep her in, and all was quiet again and they were a happy donkey family, except of course at mealtimes when they would always bite and kick each other.

Cherry Blossom resembles a whale. 'Is that donkey pregnant?' is a frequent enquiry. 'No, she's not, she's just fat, she eats everything,' is my usual reply. In the recently published donkey sanctuary books, it tells you how very careful you have to be with their diet as it is so easy for them to get colic and die. Maybe through years of eating sticky buns and wooden garden sheds, Cherry has grown a cast-iron stomach – she can eat anything: nettles, docks, custard pies, ham sandwiches, chocolate éclairs. One day I found her eating the blue plastic lining of the stable roof and tried to get it away from her in a tug of war which I lost; it all disappeared down her throat. The next morning I expected to find a dead donkey, but no, there she was cheerfully grazing alongside Henry looking none the worse for her blue vinyl meal.

Happily when her season ended she remained in love and, with Frances so wrapped up in her daughter, Henry and Cherry became inseparable, so inseparable that to this day nothing will keep them apart.

As Artistic Director, Patrick felt he was entitled to a moment of nepotism and requested that Henry and Cherry Blossom audition for a non-speaking role in *As You Like It* as an ass in the forest of Arden accompanying Celia and Rosalind, but there was hot competition in the shape of two donkeys nominated by Mr Lingfield.

Henry went on stage without a murmur to do a scene with the actor Ronnie Stevens playing Touchstone. All was going very well until, in the wings, Cherry Blossom became thoroughly enraged at the separation: 'Hee-haw, hee-haw,' she went on incessantly and Henry in turn answered back – 'Hee-haw, hee-haw' – totally drowning out the actor's lines.

'This really won't do at all,' said Ronnie, so despite the nepotism, Jacko, Mr Lingfield's donkey, got the part and Henry and Cherry Blossom were sent home jubilant that they had succeeded in *not* getting the role. However, Jacko disgraced himself on the first night and Ronnie Stevens had to clear it all up in full view of a hysterical audience. Serve him right, Henry would never have done a thing like that!

Next time, when a donkey was required for *Victory*,

Patrick's adaptation of Thomas Hardy's *The Dynasts*, at the theatre, Henry was awarded the role without auditioning. Every night he would co-star with Rosie, the grey pony from up the road, who played Napoleon's (James Bolam's) mount, and they both acted out their parts to perfection.

Eventually, Henry's career seemed to come full circle. *Joseph and His Technicolour Dreamcoat* visited Chichester and upon its becoming known that Henry was already familiar with the role, having played it at Eastbourne before he came to us, he was immediately cast and excelled himself in the part with bravura.

On none of these occasions did Henry receive payment, but he did demand, through his agent, a chauffeur-driven horse-box to and from the theatre every evening for the run of the play. He is now 'resting', back to idling away his time with the others. Perhaps if *Jesus Christ Superstar* comes round again, his crowning glory as the traditional bearer of Jesus into Jerusalem will arrive.

Mr Lingfield, the donkey man, lost his picturesque fields on the Chichester by-pass to a new housing estate and I suppose Patrick could count himself lucky that by now we had only just enough pasture for four sets of hooves as I would sorely have liked to rescue Mr Lingfield's forty donkeys from an unsure outcome at the Cattle Market.

As a result of Mr Lingfield's going out of the donkey business word went around that we had donkeys that children could ride. Phoebe couldn't be ridden until she was three, but she was trained very early and was such a big hit with the children that she always went along for the trip anyway. Also, a donkey left behind is a pathetic and noisy sight. The hospice, the schools, St Richard's Hospital, the local villages, the churches – there was hardly a fête that didn't request their services and during the summer months I kept a diary exclusively for them. However, even lending a donkey for charity rides had its problems and my RSPCA friend advised me to have a sign reading:

AT YOUR OWN RISK.

VOLUNTARY CONTRIBUTIONS.

In fact they are always kept insured anyway because there is always a chance of the unexpected. Once a dog on a lead jumped up at a donkey giving a ride. The donkey reared, the child came off but was caught by me, so all was well on that occasion, but you can never afford to be lax for one moment. The 'voluntary contributions' obviates the necessity to have a licence to give rides. It's a nuisance but necessary for all that.

One day, when Mr Lingfield called by to cut back the donkeys' hooves (a six-weekly occurrence) he commented on Cherry Blossom's feet. 'You'll have to be careful, she's got seedy toe,' he said. 'With wet conditions it could turn into foot-rot if you're not very careful.'

6

How to Tell a Quack
from a *Quack*

It was with foot-rot in mind that I took another look at the smaller paddock which was frequently flooded.

We had been fascinated by an aerial photograph of Poplars, revealing a large round circle in the small front paddock. Could it have been the relic of a monastic fish pond, we asked ourselves? This, combined with the fact that the ground was permanently muddy and wet, persuaded us to transform it into a duck pond with an island with a willow tree in the middle of it. Mike Bridger, our neighbouring farmer, duly arrived with his tractor to dig it out and bank it, and, much to our delight, the venture proved less complicated than we had feared. The bottom of the pond turned out to be clay and held water naturally so there was no need for an expensive black vinyl liner. However, even with the aid of our metal detector, the anticipated hoard of Roman coins never materialized, and the old bedstead, horse-shoes and countless oyster shells proved to be of no value whatsoever. Of monastic fish-pond relics, there was no sign.

No sooner had the pond been dug than I received a call from Mr Aves up the road. He was moving house and wanted a good home for his ducks and coop. I was only too pleased to offer them sanctuary, and two little white Aylesbury ducks arrived with five Khaki Campbells. Soon afterwards Min Flower at Cat Rescue called up to see if I wanted a white Aylesbury drake and some more Khaki Campbells and, thinking they would get on in perfect harmony with those from Mr Aves, I agreed to take them on. A total amateur at ducks, I was soon to learn the hard way about their mores and sex life. Drakes normally have one special mate, but this attachment does not stop them from having endless affairs with other ducks, or indeed other drakes' wives, even if this causes the odd fight. I soon had a bunch of battered females – technically called 'draked'. An advisable ratio is four ducks to one drake, and I had one to one, so something had to be done. Fortunately, Dick Harmer, our bird-mad friend from up the road, came to the rescue.

'I've sixteen white Aylesbury ducklings that I bought at the market sitting in a box on my kitchen table. How would you like all the females?' he said.

'That would be wonderful,' I replied. 'But do you know how to sex them at such a young age?'

'Easy,' Dick said, 'you can tell the females from the males by their voices.'

Sure enough, when I went up to collect them he picked all the ducks out by their guttural voices – at last my battered duck problem would be solved.

However, it didn't take long for me to realize that something was seriously amiss. At feeding time the newcomers chased away my drakes, very peculiar behaviour for females. I consulted the local chicken and duck farmer, Graham Pitt, and he came over to look.

'Those Aylesburies are all drakes,' he pronounced, 'but it is quite difficult to tell. Your friend is right, you do sex them by their voices, but it's the opposite of what you would expect. The drakes have the croaky "quack" and the ducks have the deep bass "*quack*".' I thanked Graham very much for his judgement, but saw that I could now have an even greater problem on my hands. Either I would have to set up a hospital for extremely battered ducks or I would have to form a gay drake colony.

'Dick, you know those ducks you gave me, I'm sorry to have to tell you they're all drakes.'

'No problem,' said Dick. 'I still have the other eight – they must be females, so we'll just do a switch.' With a heavy heart I handed over the eight white drakes to an uncertain fate, but at least my drake–duck ratio was remedied at last, or so I thought. The trouble was, as with the human race, certain ducks were more attractive to drakes than others. To you and me they might look equally beautiful, but not to a drake. Thus the one I called Brigitte Bardot was so over-mated in the season that she had to be isolated for her own protection, while other Plain Janes didn't have any luck at all!

It was during this time that I joined the committee of the Brent Lodge Wild Bird Hospital at the instigation of the warden, Dennis Fenter, and set about helping the wild duck population. Dennis has such a continuous intake of various birds that a large part of his work involves finding homes for them after he has successfully restored them to health. They may be victims of oil spills, or of fishermen, whose hooks have to be removed under anaesthetic, or of car accidents or of other animals, like cats and dogs. With our large pond and its island I was able to offer a haven to several one-winged or one-legged mallards to feed alongside my domestic ducks. However, much to my horror their numbers slowly diminished and we soon realized we had a local fox. This presented something of a moral dilemma: humans ate the odd chicken, so was it right to begrudge Mrs Fox and her family the odd duck? I certainly wouldn't have harmed the vixen, so it was up to me to remedy the situation.

But, no matter how hard I tried to catch my crippled ducks to put them in at night, I never succeeded. Fortunately, before Mrs Fox chomped her way through all of them, they managed to hatch out ducklings, which was thrilling. One duck had ten ducklings, one duck had nine, another had only one. Tragically, one day the duck with the solitary duckling lost it – it simply disappeared – and the wailing noise she made that day was heartrending. The other two mother ducks, however, took compassion on her, and allowed her to join their families. They formed a crèche and while one would go walkabout, the other two would look after the babies. The next problem on the horizon was that there was no one among the invalid adult ducks to teach them to fly. When the young ones did try, their attempts were very comical and often we had to *duck* as they flew by just managing to skim past chimneys and telephone wires. The solution to safe-guarding the ducklings was to let Sophie sleep outside with them. Kipling, her son, was so thick he would probably have eaten the odd one himself, but Sophie understood what her task was and could frequently be heard growling or barking as she prowled along the perimeter of our boundary through the night. Proof of how good she was at the job was that by the time the weather grew cold and she would not sleep outside any longer all the ducklings had met other wild ducks and flown away.

One evening in mid-winter when the pond finally froze over there remained only one solitary crippled mallard, and I despaired for his future. However, that night, perhaps conscious of his own predicament, he followed the domestic ducks into their coop, and has been doing so ever since. He appropriated a Khaki Campbell wife, no longer considered himself a mallard and would have nothing to do with the visiting wild duck population at all.

From time to time people would ring up with ducks they wanted re-homing. One such was Mr Golding from Selsey who had a mallard female he had rescued.

'Are her wings clipped?' I asked. 'Because otherwise she'll just fly away.'

'We'll bring her in a cat basket and leave it beside the pond for half an hour. At the end of that time she'll be so pleased to see other ducks she'll join them,' said Mr Golding.

'Are you sure?' said I, as this theory did not accord with the six-week home acceptance period Mr Fenter had spoken of.

'Of course,' said Mr Golding, with great conviction.

With a cup of tea in hand we stared at the basket and after thirty minutes had elapsed, we let her out. She took one cursory look at the other ducks, took off, wheeled overhead and vanished into the distance, never to be seen again.

'Well, I never,' said Mr Golding.

The following year some of our grown-up mallard ducklings came back to have their own families. It was interesting to see that this time the crèche didn't exist and it was the fathers and mothers in turn who looked after their families, not just the mums. By now we have raised many young ducklings and in the winter there is nothing more thrilling than seeing the wild ducks converging on Poplars in the evening, gliding over the roof and skidding to a halt on the pond, where they know they will be assured of a meal, no matter what the weather.

On the domestic front we increased the population with some Magpie ducks (so-called because they are black and white like magpies) and some Indian Runner ducks who make us laugh; they walk in such an upright fashion they remind us of Charlie Chaplin! However, I did continue to make mistakes: I once bought two very beautiful North Carolina ducks at vast expense, but with their wings clipped and refusing to go in at night they had vanished by the next day. And I accepted another Magpie drake from Dennis Fenter at the bird hospital, but it turned out to be such a sex maniac, jumping on anything, male or female, all day, and causing such havoc, that none of the ducks would go into the coop with him at night. I had to admit defeat and the bisexual Magpie was returned to Dennis.

Unless a domestic duck sits on eggs in the coop where it is safe, we don't allow the ducks to lay in the garden where they can be eaten. However, one year we found a Khaki Campbell sitting on eggs near the barn and we managed to construct an anti-fox cage around her. Unfortunately she had appropriated the eggs of a wild mallard who had obviously met that fate already, and they proved to be cold and dead. We managed to substitute the clutch with eggs from our various ducks and she continued to sit on them for another month, but slowly one by one she removed them and they were dead inside. Eventually there were none left, and the duck was severely traumatized. For two weeks afterwards she quacked inconsolably round the nest and had to be forced back into the coop with the other ducks at night. Eventually she recovered, but her distress and the misery of the wild duck who lost her only duckling were not easily forgotten.

Then two of our domestic ducks decided to sit on eggs. One brown Khaki Campbell sat on the safe nest in the barn, and the other, an Indian Runner, was clever enough to build a nest in her coop where she was protected. However, there was a very strange phenomenon, her nest kept on getting higher and higher, like adding tier upon tier to a wedding cake, as she stole all the eggs daily from the other ducks to add to her own.

*

That week I had a dinner party and one of the interesting guests was Oliver Graham-Jones, the vet from Regent's Park Zoo, now living locally. He regaled us all evening with tales of his famous patients and explained how, in the course of his term there he had managed to improve the lot of a number of the animals. When he had first arrived the operating facilities were very primitive; merely a large box into which the animal was put while the anaesthetic gas was pumped in through a small hole. One day Chomley, the chimpanzee, had to have an operation and Oliver Graham-Jones and his team were astounded when after the usual ten minutes had elapsed Chomley was looking as lively as ever. After twenty minutes he was still showing no signs of the anaesthetic whereas the vet and his team were feeling distinctly woozy. They examined all the equipment and there was nothing wrong with it, but when they took a closer look at Chomley they discovered he was sitting there quite happy with his finger up the anaesthetic tube!

He also told me of a little old lady client with a stray cat she had befriended. He was a mangy old thing and she was totally devoted to him. One day she called Oliver and told him the cat was very ill and he went straight over to see her. Tommy, as she called him, was in fact not only very ill, he was dying, and there was nothing Oliver could do to help other than offer to take the body away.

'Is that what usually happens?' she asked sorrowfully.

'Yes,' he replied, 'and I send them off to an animal crematorium.'

The deed was done and Tommy did go off to the animal crematorium where he was hygienically disposed of. However, six weeks later Oliver Graham-Jones had another call from the little old lady.

'I've been thinking,' she said. 'I really would like Tommy's ashes back for a proper burial, the grave has been dug by his favourite rose bush in the garden, and my vicar has offered to say a few words for him.' Oliver was appalled, he had not asked for the ashes to be returned and after six weeks there was no possible way of getting them back, but she was so earnest he found himself saying: 'Of course, I'll bring Tommy's remains over tomorrow.' Alone in the surgery, pondering his predicament, he spotted an old parrot skeleton suspended from the ceiling. He cut it down and with a mortar and pestle got to work. When that was finished he got a shovel and picked up some of the wood ash from his log fire. He fetched a shoe box and mixed the crushed parrot bones and wood ash together.

The next day he delivered the package to the little old lady who was thrilled to get Tommy back. Two days later he was invited to the funeral service. The grave had been properly dug and was lined with green baize, a few friends had been invited, and the vicar conducted the little service with proper decorum.

Oliver felt terrible, thinking of the parrot and the wood ash, but he was in too deep to tell the truth. The next day she rang him wanting to know how to get an engraved marble headstone for Tommy. Oliver explained that it would be very expensive, but she said that nothing was too good for Tommy.

A few days later he stopped by, and saw an umbrella over the grave.

'You see, Tommy never liked the rain, and I wouldn't like him to get wet,' she said.

Until then Oliver had still had his doubts about the parrot, but now he knew he had done the right thing, he had made the little old lady very happy.

*

When I consulted Oliver myself about my Indian Runner sitting on her wedding cake nest, he explained that she had an excessive amount of hormones and that as she couldn't keep so many eggs warm, sadly it would be unlikely they would ever hatch out. They didn't and, for some unknown reason, neither did those of the duck in the barn, and having one by one ascertained their eggs were dead they both stopped sitting on the same day. Both were highly distraught, quacking frenziedly, and that night I took the Khaki Campbell from the barn and put her inside with the others. Feathers flew everywhere as the two distressed ducks flew at each other, each recognizing the maternal jealousies of the other, and they had to be separated until they were back to normal again.

One day when we were about to go on holiday I noticed the ducks had dark circles under their eyes, and instinctively knew they were ill. I rushed one to Dennis Fenter who diagnosed dehydration and diarrhoea due to our unfamiliar hot summer. He immediately came to the rescue and insisted on taking them all to his hospital for treatment for our entire holiday. What a friend! By the time we came back they were all restored to perfect health. Now they are fed Dennis's recommended dog food twice a week for extra vitamins and the open coops are in aviaries along with a permanent supply of water.

Another illness ducks frequently suffer from in the summer is bumble foot caused by the hard ground. A form of corn on the underside of their webbed feet, it causes them to hobble about painfully when there are long dry periods. Ironically this is the period when the donkeys race around, cavorting on the firm soil.

The reverse is true in winter when the ducks glory in mud and splash about in puddles on wet days, while the poor old donkeys stand hunched in their shelters gazing

out at the soggy fields, possibly contemplating the likeli-
hood of impending foot-rot!

When we came back from our vacation I asked Dennis
Fenter about our spectacular lack of success with duck
breeding. He explained that domestic ducks are not very
good sitters.

'You could get an incubator, but they're expensive –
most duck-keepers prefer a broody hen as a mother. Why
don't you get yourself one? It would be much easier,' he
said.

So when I visited Mrs Powell at Rowlands Castle to
collect some Rouen and Buff Orpington ducks, I took
notice of some very pretty small hens with feathered leg-
gings.

'They are Silkie Bantam hens,' said Mrs Powell. 'They
make particularly good broodies.' I had already, in passing, broached the subject of hens with Patrick but had
never been particularly enchanted by them. These little
birds were quite different.

'Do you sell them?' I asked.

'Yes,' said Mrs Powell. 'I could let you have a trio, a
cockerel and two hens.' She indicated one beautiful white
cockerel and two pretty brown hens, and these we put in
an aerated box alongside those containing the various
ducks. Luckily, I had had the foresight to ask Jim King to
make a small section of the aviary separate from the
ducks (for an emergency) and I deposited the bantams
there when I got them home.

Hens boring? Never was I more wrong; they rush
towards you doing balletic grands jetés and like nothing
better than a cuddle. I called them Rudolph, Darcy
Bushell, and Natalia Makarova after the ballet dancers,
so graceful were they. On the practical side the little pul-
lets' eggs were so delicious we all fought over them. One

morning I nearly came to blows with my mother who had appropriated six Silkie eggs and hidden them in her car. I had calculated there were just enough eggs for our guests and ourselves at breakfast. In the event there were enough for them, but Patrick and I just sat munching our toast and marmalade!

The other incredibly fortunate plus was that our beautiful cockerel didn't crow, although occasionally he would manage a faint 'doddle-doo'. However, to our sorrow, he died of a heart attack a few months later. I think his 'doodle-doo' was indicative of his state of health; obviously, he had not been well for some time.

'Mrs Powell, do you by any chance have another Silkie cockerel you can spare?' She did, and off I went to collect him. There is never any shortage of available cock birds as two adult cocks will fight, although a cock chick will sometimes be accepted by his cock dad. The new Silkie cockerel was definitely very butch, and was called Irek after the Royal Ballet dancer. The two hens found him rather attractive too and clucked all round him. The noise was deafening: 'Cock-a-doodle-doo, cock-a-doodle-doo, cock-a-doodle-doo,' went our macho cock at sunrise; we longed for our old cockerel. However, on the positive side, both our neighbours seemed deaf to his crowing, and you get used to the sound of your own animals. The main problem occurs when we have guests; I become so aware of the crowing of the cock, quacking of the ducks, braying of the donkeys, and barking of the dogs that I get up terribly early to let them all out. Good days are rainy days when most of them take cover and silence reigns.

As I was unable to find any more Silkie hens and the demand for eggs was insatiable I decided to let both hens sit and put extra duck eggs under them in the hope they might make better mothers than the ducks. After a month one hen hatched out one little white chick and abandoned the rest of the eggs. This I'm told is often the right thing for them to do. They should look after the living baby rather than ignore it to hatch out more eggs. The best solution is to take the catch of the day from all the hens or ducks and put them all under the sitting bird so they hatch out all at once. The other hen sitting on duck eggs hatched out a tiny yellow duckling and two days later it was dead. I removed the cockerel, and the hen with the chick, and she hatched out another duckling. Two days later it too was dead, pecked to death. I presumed that the poor hen was so upset at seeing her 'chick' with deformed webbed feet that she had decided to put it out of its misery. However, it was no such thing, as a few days later she tried to kill the other hen's chick. We now no longer called her Natalia but 'The Murderess' or 'Lady Macbeth'. Frank Page, Mrs Powell's poultry fancier, said in such cases poultry farmers would just cut off their beaks. But as she was the most affectionate of the hens – to humans – we kept her on unmutilated, despite her psychotic behaviour. However, we did have to separate her from the other ducklings and chicks.

The demand for the eggs was still insatiable and I was very pleased when poor Mrs Powell rang me up and offered me two more hens. A fox had managed to get into her fox-proof run, and not wanting to re-wire the entire area, she was looking for homes for the survivors. My delight was more than matched by that of the cockerel who set about making them feel at home immediately!

In the daytime when the hens are foraging around the paddock, one of them will often come to find you and lead you back to the aviary and coops. If you let her in she invariably lays an egg and starts to coo and cluck and screech very excitedly to let the world know she has done it. That immediately sets the cockerel off on an extended 'cock-a-doodle-doo' telling us how clever he's been too. With four hens as wives, Irek has grown even noisier, but then it would seem he has more to crow about!

7

Friendly Ferrets and an Unreliable Pigeon

The downside of keeping poultry was the rats. Our cat population kept them down in the barn, but as we had to keep the fox out of the aviaries at night, the cats couldn't get in either. Rats are ingenious: they tunnel under the cement, weakening the foundations, and break in just under the coops, where they have ready access to the grain. We tried *everything*. Humane rat traps they totally ignored, and ordinary rat traps they would simply operate in such a way that they snatched the cheese or meat without getting caught.

Finally, when my white Silkie cockerel was bitten by a rat, I resorted to more desperate means: poison. It was against my better judgement as the death it causes is so horrid, but I couldn't see any other way. The lethal powder was mixed with corn and put in rat-accessible-only places, like old pipes. It worked a treat and we wiped out a whole rat family. Resilient as ever, they came back, only this time they rejected the corn-poison mixture.

'Try mixing it with drinking chocolate,' said Bob the gardener. 'They can't resist that.' He was right, once again the poor rats met an unpleasant fate.

Occasionally, I would help Monique's Cat and Rabbit Rescue, a local charity, with their fund-raising. One particular evening they were holding a murder-mystery dinner, and one of the guests, during an interval, was regaling us with the sex life of the stick insect. She was also an expert on rats.

'What you need, to keep them away, are ferret droppings,' she said. 'Rats consider ferrets to be superior and give them a wide berth.' I registered that particular piece of information but rejected it: where on earth was I going to get ferret droppings? I certainly didn't want a live ferret, they were nasty, vicious, bitey creatures.

A week later Monique called me to thank me for my participation as the narrator in her murder mystery.

'You'll never guess what,' she said, 'a ferret has turned up here. Awfully sweet, very licky, but Rabbit Rescue is hardly the place for a ferret to reside, is it?'

I reminded Patrick of our on-going rat problem and broached the subject of the ferret.

'I know you, it's just a ruse to get another animal,' he said. 'Besides, they're vicious little creatures, with razor-sharp teeth.'

'This one's a girl, very sweet and gives kisses, but the point is they really do keep away rats,' I insisted.

'Are you sure?' Patrick looked doubtful.

'Positive,' I replied, hoping against hope that the piece of country folk-lore I had heard would prove true . . .!

She was gorgeous, with the lilac colouring of a Siamese cat. When I picked her up she made little happy clicking noises, and gave tiny moist licks. I had heard ferrets stank as well, but she had rather a sweet musk smell.

'Would you mind if I took her?' I asked Monique.

'Not at all,' she replied. 'It'll be a relief to get her away from all these bunnies.'

'What should I feed her on?' I asked.

'We've been giving her cat food, she seemed to like it.'

At home, Jim King had prepared a rabbit hutch for her, with double locks, and had lined it with metal mesh to prevent an escape. She would live in the chicken aviary, but have the full run of the enclosure when the hens were let out each day.

I named her Fanny, after Fanny Sitwell described as small with tiny hands and feet in the biography of Robert Louis Stevenson that I was reading at the time.

So far so good, ferret keeping was obviously easy. I called my old school-friend Snooky, from Brighton schooldays – I knew her sons had kept ferrets.

'You've got a ferret!' Snooky replied in disbelief. 'Well, they are remarkable; when we lost ours twenty-five miles away, staying with friends, he even found his own way home.'

'It's a girl ferret,' I said. There was silence the other end.

'Oh,' she said, 'that's not such good news: when the females come into season, if they're not mated, they die.'

'Thanks a lot,' I said. 'So either I have lots of baby ferrets, which I need like a hole in the head, or a dead ferret.' Still, I was grateful for the information and set about locating the telephone number of Ferret Rescue, which I had seen pinned up in one of the animal supply stores.

Finally I rang Roger Sked, the head of Ferret Rescue.

'I've been given a little girl ferret that turned up at Cat and Rabbit Rescue and I wondered if you could give me some advice?'

'Of course,' he said. 'Why don't I come and see you?'

My first impression of Roger Sked was that he looked just like a handsome ferret himself, fine boned and slim with a long, pointed face and little twinkly eyes.

'I'm so glad you have a ferret,' he said. 'They're a lot like your dobermanns – they have a terrible reputation, often totally unfounded.'

'Yes, it's been quite a surprise to find that she's so gentle and sweet,' I agreed. 'I had no idea. I am concerned though,' I continued, 'a friend told me female ferrets die if they're not mated. Surely that can't be true?'

'I'm afraid they can do,' he said, 'but there are different solutions, the main ones being spaying or jills jabs, personally I prefer the latter for my girls.'

The 'girls' he was talking about turned out to be four polecat ferrets which he frequently took out on walks with leads and harnesses.

'There are hobbs, males, and they can be fierce if they are used exclusively for hunting; hobbles, neutered males, are often very good-natured, and jills, females, are usually just as sweet as your ferret.'

When I brought Fanny in he pronounced her 'an excellent specimen', but added, 'You really should have two.'

'Two?' I choked. 'Why?'

'Females get on very well together – you can keep several – and it is very important in winter that they don't lose their body heat.' Fanny's hutch was full of straw, but I had to admit that in January or February it might not be a bad thing to be curled up with another ferret.

'In the summer,' he said, 'they mustn't get too hot, so don't leave them out in the sun or they will overheat.'

Ferret keeping was sounding less simple by the minute.

'Anything else I should know?'

'Yes, they can get anaemic, so they should have liver from time to time – and mice with fur, or birds with feathers, which are good for their digestion,' he explained.

'Where on earth am I going to find small dead animals with fur or feathered birds?' I said aghast. 'So far I've given her just cat food.'

'It's OK as a temporary measure, but you should supplement that at least with frozen day-old chicks,' he said. I had heard about those day-old chicks – it had been the reason I had not wanted a tame barn owl, but now it seemed there was no going back.

'It is a humane way of dealing with too many cockerels.'

I was a little comforted – I knew from my own experience that too many cockerels would be a problem, and if they were going to keep my ferret alive . . .

'You really should have two girls you know,' he returned to his original subject. 'It just so happens that I have a pair of jills in my car . . .'

'I couldn't possibly have anything that wasn't as sweet as mine,' I said warily, thinking of Patrick's reaction.

'They're just a few months old and even tamer,' he assured me.

One was exactly like mine, the other was a young albino ferret, pale cream in colour, with red eyes, apparently the purer in breeding. She was adorable, grunting with pleasure at being handled and showering me with little kisses.

'Are you sure they'll get on?' I said, somewhat won over by this lovable creature. 'Definitely,' he replied. 'Though you must start them off in separate hutches. They will get together at their own pace, but by tomorrow you will find them curled up together. They also love going down tubes. In fact builders use them to take through conduit wires – they just put a dead rabbit at the other end of the pipe.'

'Anything else I should know?' I asked. I had learnt quite enough for one evening.

'Yes, one thing,' he said. 'They catch human diseases – flu, colds – in fact, that's why the poor things are so popular in laboratory experiments. So keep away if you're ill, or wear a mask.'

When I peeked in next day they were happily playing tag through cardboard tubes and by that evening the two were entwined, curled up together in Fanny's nest, firm friends. I resolved to call the albino Fanny Two, or Fanny Osbourne after R.L. Stevenson's wife, who also had small hands and feet.

The by-product was the ferret droppings in the wood-shavings. Bob the gardener sprinkled them all around the poultry cages and the rats disappeared at last! Even Patrick expressed his approval of the two Fannies.

The peculiar thing about animal rescue is that very often, without you looking for them, the animals just turn up. One day I was sitting in the conservatory enjoying a rare moment of tranquillity when a racing pigeon walked in through the open door.

That's not a very good idea, Mr Pigeon, I thought. There are cats and dogs around here who could turn you into ferret fodder if you are not careful! Mr Pigeon didn't seem at all perturbed as I walked towards him and picked him up, he was obviously used to being handled. However, what was I to do with him? He needed to be fed and watered and kept somewhere safe, as he was clearly rather exhausted from what must have been a long flight.

I decided to put him in a spare aviary with a couple of temporary perches. I placed some mixed corn and some water in cat bowls on top of a large hutch and the pigeon settled in very happily. He had evidently come from a comfortable home as he tucked himself away in the hutch for the night in the straw.

What was I to do about Mr Pigeon in the long term? I decided to call up my friend, Richard Harmer, a bird expert.

'A racing pigeon?' Dick repeated.

'Yes,' I said, 'and it has proper identity tags with letters and numbers attached to its feet. At the moment it is in a cage, but it can't stay there for ever.'

'You could do some research through the Pigeon Fanciers and find out where he comes from, but personally I wouldn't bother.'

'Why not?' I said, surprised, Dick was usually conscientious, and practical.

'They will ask you where you found him, the date and time and then you will say, "Would you like him back?" and they will say "No, he is an unreliable pigeon".'

'Surely people should feel a responsibility towards their birds?' I said.

'Yes, they should,' said Richard, 'but I assure you a homing pigeon that won't fly home is not wanted.'

I was perplexed – maybe if I did release him in our front paddock he would go home. Maybe. It was risky, given the number of predators around, but I finally determined to try. I picked him up easily and threw him into the air; away he went up on to the roof and then disappeared from sight. I was so relieved, finally Mr Pigeon had found his way home.

I went indoors to make a cup of tea for Patrick and myself, and we went into the conservatory for fifteen minutes' quiet conversation. It was five o'clock. At five-fifteen precisely the racing pigeon strolled back into the conservatory. Once again I picked him up and put him in the cage. What a dilemma! It took me a couple of days to decide what to do next, he seemed so happy and there was no great urgency, but I was determined that he should have a better, freer life than the one we afforded him.

I decided to drive with him a few miles up the lane and release him from there. He set off in the direction of the North of England . . . and was at Poplars waiting for me in the crab apple tree just outside the conservatory when I got home. I went and picked him up and replaced him once again in the aviary.

Not one to be easily defeated, I rang Dennis Fenter of the Brent Lodge Bird Hospital. 'Dennis, I wonder if you could possibly do me a favour. I have rescued a racing pigeon, but I need to release it somewhere safe. If he stays around here he is so tame he is going to get pounced on by my cats. Could he possibly stay with you?'

'Of course,' said Dennis. 'In fact, we have had a lot of exhausted racing pigeons brought in to us recently, and at least if he sticks around here he'll be fed. However, I don't think that's likely. My bet is he'll be home before you.'

My heart sank, maybe I should release Mr Pigeon in Trafalgar Square instead; it would be harder for him to find his way home to Poplars from there and the tourists would feed him. However, for the moment, the bird hospital seemed the best option. I arrived at 2 p.m. and Dennis, a large, smiling bear of a man, came out to greet me.

'I wish you luck,' he chortled, 'but if you have had him a few days the odds are he'll be back at your home before you can switch on the car engine.'

'Oh well, I don't hold out much hope but I have to try.' With that I took Mr Pigeon in my hands and threw him up in the air. He circled around the bird hospital getting his bearings and finally flew off . . . towards the hills in the opposite direction to Poplars Farm House.

'He's done it!' I said excitedly. 'He's a bit late, but he isn't an unreliable pigeon after all!'

'Well, I'll be damned!' exclaimed Dennis. 'That's most unusual.'

On the drive home through the country lanes my euphoria left me; I realized I was going to miss my cheeky racing pigeon. Back home at about five o'clock as I was boiling the kettle for some tea I suddenly heard a shout from Patrick: 'Your blasted pigeon's back!'

And sure enough, there he was once again in the crab apple tree. It had taken him three hours to find his way back to Poplars, a distance of six miles, but Dennis Fenter had been right and as far as *we* were concerned he was a reliable pigeon after all!

8

Too Many Feet for Too Little Pasture

As it happened, the racing pigeon survived both cats and dogs.

We had kept the right dobermann puppy as Kipling would never have caught him anyway. His brother Barnaby, as the Fressons called him, was extremely intelligent – just like Sophie, his mother – and two of them in the family would have been unbearable. Also, Barnaby was wont to howl to get them up early in the morning, and there was no fence or gate known to humanity that would keep him in.

Kipling, the dim-witted brother, didn't even work out for himself that he could effortlessly jump over our four-foot wall, and we didn't enlighten him. Sophie thus remained top dog, which she would not have done with Barnaby, who had always got the better of her even when he was a tiny pup, while Kipling, although stronger, was generally submissive. The Fressons also had a male retriever they'd rescued, and without a bitch about the two dogs co-existed very harmoniously.

So far, our two males had lived together very happily with Sophie. However, we were to rue the day that we thought we knew better than the Dobermann Club. 'You can't keep a male dobermann,' they had assured me, 'with another male, of any breed, together with a bitch.'

It was one sunny Sunday morning, the dogs were

whining, and we wanted to have a lazy morning in bed, so we agreed to let the dogs upstairs for a treat. Sophie leapt on to the bottom of the bed, followed by Kipling. Ben then clambered up on my side of the bed and that was when suddenly all hell broke loose: Kipling thrust out at Ben, and savaged him. Screaming, I pulled Kipling off Ben by the neck, with a large chunk of white hair in his mouth, while Patrick hastily bundled a bewildered and cowed Ben into another room. And that's how we lived, in a suddenly transformed state of siege, with Kipling determined to kill Ben if he came anywhere near one of us or Sophie. Poor Ben, he was such a gentle-natured dog that we were reluctant to lose him. However, Mother came to the rescue – she had always thought he was such a perfect, well-mannered dog – so he went to live contentedly with my parents in Hove. Kipling, on the other hand, was becoming a 'problem' dog, so we had to keep him. He refused to allow any dog, of either sex, other than Sophie, in the house and had the same unsociable attitude on walks on the beach or through the fields. We were forced, for our own peace of mind, and the safety of other people's pets, to get him a muzzle, but since he came to associate it with walks, he accepted it readily. Fortunately, his relationship with human beings was never in doubt; he adored people and could sit being patted by them for hours.

Often on a winter's evening, despite the central heating, Sophie would stand in front of the electric fire and whine at us: 'Will you please put the fire on for me.' While she settled down peacefully in front of it, Kipling would profit from the occasion and go and take over her bed. Half an hour later, by now far too hot, she would come in and whimper pathetically: 'Kipling's on *my* bean bag,' and demand that he be ejected and moved to his own bed. Mission accomplished, she would then demand to be covered with her blanket, tucked in, and lulled by the sweet sounds of 'good girl, beautiful girl' she would utter moans of ecstasy before drifting into a state of canine contentment.

Before Mr Vinnicombe the vet had spayed Sophie she was already obsessive about her food, after the operation she became ten times worse. Not only would she scavenge on walks, finding the most putrid myxie-ridden rabbit corpses, but nothing left on kitchen surfaces would be safe.

We were now one dog down, and soon, sadly, we were to lose a cat. Early one morning, there was a frightening squeal of brakes in our country lane. I rushed out to find Whitey, scourge of rats, lying dead in the road outside the house next door, victim of a hit-and-run driver.

I was very upset, and very angry – particularly as the odds were that Kim had probably been killed by a car as well. People were constantly treating our narrow country lane as though it were a race track, without any thought for pets or wildlife. My neighbour, Mrs Jones, was pretty irate as well, as she had lost two cats in the previous six months. Finally, a speed-merchant removed the bonnet of her nanny's car as it crept out of her driveway. The nanny turned out to be the daughter of a policeman, and we therefore called in the police, who resolved to monitor the cars down our road for a week.

'On Tuesday eight cars came down here at eighty miles an hour,' said the Inspector.

'But two cars can't even pass in opposite directions at the same time . . . can't you stop them?' I asked.

'I'm afraid not,' he replied coolly.

'What about a speed limit?' I said.

'That would mean street lighting, there's not enough houses to warrant that and it's expensive,' was the answer.

With Noddy, the poodle that was *meant* to be a pony!

With Huston the Yorkie on Brighton beach.

Sweet 16 with a young Omar Sharif fresh from filming *Dr Zhivago*.

With my hero Jeremy Brett in an episode of *The Champions*.

Poplars Farmhouse.

Blue, my first dobermann.

Ben and Sophie on holiday in the Welsh mountains.

Sid Green defending his bees from my mokes! Henry (*above right*), Frances (*below left*) and Frances's foal, Phoebe.

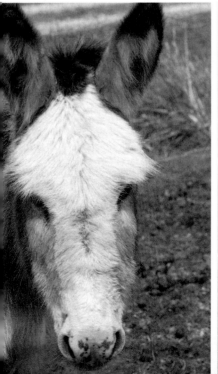

(*Clockwise from top left*) Coley the vandal, Blackie the moggie, Rex and Abbie the boiler cats.

Nureyev the cockerel (*left*) and his wife and chicks.

The arrival of the Norfolk Black turkeys caused upset in the boiler room for George/Georgina and Gertie the guinea-fowl.

The dove that loved ducks.

Mamma mallard and her brood.

The calling drake with his Khaki Campbell wife.

'What about sleeping policemen?' said I, in some desperation.

'I've got plenty of those at the station,' he replied with a sardonic smile, 'but, no, not the kind you mean, too many motorcyclists would come a cropper.'

After exploring all the possibilities a compromise was reached: the council would pay for horse riding signs because of the volume of riders in our area and I would pay them privately for two wild fowl signs just opposite, to try to deter people from squashing our moorhens and mallard ducklings, not to mention the cats. It wasn't very satisfactory, but the best that could be achieved in the circumstances.

Meanwhile, the dobermanns were delighted at Whitey's absence, while Blackie, whom they speedily took to intimidating, was inconsolable. He spent all day outside, looking for Whitey and would miaow piteously around the house, he so missed his guardian. Patrick advised against any more cats but agreed that I should talk to Min Flower about it. I lost no time in ringing her.

'Of course the lane is a problem,' she said, 'but that is fate, and think what a wonderful time Whitey had until then. Remember hundreds of stray cats are getting put down every day, at least with you they have a chance.'

This made me feel a lot better at the prospect of another cat so I continued: 'Of course I still have the same Sophie anti-cat problem as before.'

'Don't worry,' she replied, 'I've got a little black-and-white chap here who's bomb-proof, in fact we can't wait to get rid of him.'

So off I went to the guinea pigs and the goats (this time I found the latter less appealing as they ate my car aerial). Min introduced me to the little moggie she'd mentioned. 'I recently picked him up from Leigh Park, a rather rough area in Portsmouth where some louts were threatening to do him in.'

However, the little fellow – he was only about three months old – didn't seem fazed at all by his recent experiences, and he was meltingly beautiful. He was white and black, with both eyes lined in black, as though with thick mascara. If he had been a female, we would have called him after Elizabeth Taylor, but as it was he became known as Coley, not after the fish, but because of the kohl marking around his eyes, although in his fiercer moments he was known as 'The Vandal from Leigh Park'. Blackie was pleased at last to have a companion and an ally against the dogs. But cat relationships are very strange, and although Coley's arrival helped Blackie over the death of Whitey, things started to go wrong when Coley decided he would rather be a dog. He slept with them, walked with them, ate dog food, begged for dog biscuits, like a little squirrel, and, when he wanted your attention even barked like them. Poor Blackie was really left out in the cold, but, as a resilient plebeian cat, he got on with his life of ratting and mousing as proper farm cats should.

Much to Patrick's chagrin, my friendship with Min progressed by leaps and bounds and I tried to help a little with Cat Rescue, passing stray cats on to her, and occasionally finding homes for them. On one occasion someone rang up who had seen my old ad, which was still in the local shop window, and said they had a stray cat that sounded like Kim. He wasn't at all like him, but was the identical twin of Blackie, and I decided to take him home. Blackie, who had never taken against any cat I had brought home before, or since, took one look at his twin and went berserk, trying to tear the poor creature apart.

'What do you expect?' said Patrick. 'I would complain

too if you introduced another man like me into this household!'

Twin Blackie was found a home at some stables nearby, but I was shortly to find that it was a mistake to ignore Min's advice. She had always warned me that you couldn't re-home a cat within a six-mile radius of where you discovered it as it would always find its way back. Within six weeks that is exactly what happened and we had to go and rescue him all over again. Fortunately his owner was so fond of him by then that she decided to take him back to her own house which was sufficiently far away, so Blackie Number Two was happy in the end.

In the course of finding cats homes, I realized that we also could give a home to a couple of wild cats in our stables and barn. Patrick was in grudging agreement provided they lived outside, in the barn . . .

Min swiftly came up with a pair who were inseparable, one was a Cornish Rex, and the other half Abyssinian and half Rex. They had both reached the age of nine months with very little human contact at all, as they had been confined in a cage at the end of a breeder's garden. This meant that they flinched from human contact and would run away whenever they saw you. However, within six weeks of being at Poplars both had been hit by cars in our lethal country lane. The resourceful Mr Vinnicombe put a steel pin in the leg of the Cornish Rex, and set in plaster the hips of the half Abyssinian, by now, with awesome originality, christened by me Rex and Abbie. Both had to be immobilized and incarcerated in a room for six weeks, by the end of which time, after a lot of tender loving care, they were no longer wild, although they remained highly suspicious of other human beings. Live in the barn after that? Of course they didn't, they had their own cat baskets by the boiler and, on Min's recommendation, in winter they even had mini electric blankets. Originally we had one for Rex's arthritic leg, but since the others were always occupying it they now had one each!

The cats weren't the only animals that were cosseted in winter. With such valuable koi carp in our pond I could not risk them freezing to death (or more correctly dying from noxious fumes from decaying matter, trapped by the ice) so I invested in a pond heater and a fibreglass 'igloo' to keep ice from forming. In summer we put in a fountain and aerating filters to keep the oxygen levels in the water high, and I even invested in a hospital pool where I could isolate sick fish. My expert friend Mark Luffman would come twice a year for a total clean-out. He would arrive with his special fish bus in tow, remove all the water with a special pump, and we would then clean out the pond by hand, often discovering newts and frogs in the process. The fish he kept in the bus tank with oxygen from an aqualung aerating the water, while he microscopically examined each fish. He then gave them all a salt bath in a bidet to disinfect them and to cleanse their gills before returning them to the water, thus avoiding any problems before they happened.

As a result we had very healthy and fertile fish – one summer I fished over three hundred baby koi out of the pond (to save them from being eaten by their parents).

When the fish breed the female needs one male to pursue her and one or more to squeeze the eggs out of her. This done the males then lay their sperm or milk over them. The fascinating outcome is that the baby fish have several parents and therefore no two are the same . . . which makes them very difficult to part with.

There was now the waterfall pond, the small ornamental pond, the wildlife pond, the large koi pond, the small fry pond in the barn . . . in fact a lake would have been a great asset!

*

Having made the small paddock over to the ducks in the form of a duck pond, because of the damp ground, I was aware that I was a little short of grazing land, and I was having to feed extra hay in the summer months to supplement their rations.

However, life in the paddocks was continuing fairly tranquilly for the four donkeys until one day I went for a walk in the fields opposite our house. The footpath was overgrown, but as the farmer of the fields behind us had been crop-spraying I chose not to take the dogs on our usual route. We hadn't been walking for long when I took a detour in the direction of two sad donkeys, Dandy and Donna. Normally they were so lonely they would rush over to see you, but on this occasion they were nowhere to be seen. I finally discovered them in their shelter; Donna slumped with her back hunched, her head drooping towards the ground, while Dandy looked on rather concerned. A further detour was called for while I went and rang their owner's doorbell.

'Excuse me, but you have a very sick donkey out there, and I think you should call a vet,' I said officiously.

'They're not mine, they're my ex-wife's and she rarely comes to see them any more,' he said. 'We're not on speaking terms.'

'Well someone's got to call the vet,' I insisted.

I was glad to learn that their vet was the same skilful Mr Vinnicombe, but the donkey was beyond rescuing and had to be put down. This left poor Dandy alone and inconsolable.

'What do you intend to do with the other donkey?' I asked.

'Some farmer has said he might have her,' said the man, sounding rather unconvinced.

'I think in the circumstances you had better bring her to me. I don't guarantee we'll keep her, but she shouldn't be left alone and we'll look after her until a good home can be found,' I said.

As she was already four years old and had never been handled, Dandy had to be dragged to us behind a tractor. The whole experience had left her very disturbed and for a week she paced up and down in a stable unable to join the others. At least there was no noise, the other donkeys seemed to recognize that here was one of their own in despair, and Dandy was too traumatized to bray. However, a nourishing breakfast of unfamiliar pony nuts and a dinner of sweet-smelling hay every day, and the company of the other four donkeys soon won her round; within a month she was indistinguishable in behaviour from the others.

But a new problem arose, as the grass and foliage wore away to dust.

'You've too many feet, for too little pasture,' said Sid Green. 'Those mokes of yours have got nothing to eat.' It was true, they were costing a fortune in supplementary hay all through the summer months, and something radical had to be done. It was while we were trying to resolve this dilemma that a newcomer, a jenny, neither welcomed, nor expected, arrived, not once or twice, but several times, and usually at three in the morning.

'Hee-haw, hee-haw' – all through the night she would talk to our donkeys over the fence, right under Mrs Green's window, and ours would answer back. In the morning I would inevitably find that some kindly passer-by had let her in, presuming she was one of ours.

The first time Sid Green was angry enough, but the twelfth time it happened, he was understandably puce with rage.

'Your wretched mokes are keeping Cath awake all night, what are you going to do about it?' said Sid.

'It's *not* my donkey,' I said. 'It's Mr Easton's, up the

road. It keeps escaping to join my donkeys, that's what all the rumpus is all about.'

'I don't care whose it is, something's got to be done about it, Cathy can't go on like this any longer.'

It was true, and neither could we, and nor could the rest of the hamlet – 'Heard your donkeys again last night' had become the usual accusatory greeting, not always good-tempered.

The problem was that Mr Easton only had *one* donkey and rather ramshackle fencing. Sufficient for a horse maybe, but not for a smart donkey, and Pepsi was clever, almost as clever as Cherry Blossom.

'Mr Easton, we're having a bit of a problem with your donkey. She's very sweet and we like her a lot, but she does keep escaping, arriving here and making a terrible racket through the night until she's let in.'

There was a long silence.

'Would you like to have her?' asked Mr Easton. 'We love her, but she's going to get run over on the lane one of these days and she is quiet when she's with yours.'

We didn't want yet another donkey, or at least Patrick didn't, but at the time it seemed the best solution for all concerned, at least Cathy would get some much-needed sleep. Pepsi who was very pretty indeed – dark chocolate brown with a white blaze on her forehead – fitted in immediately, making friends with all the others and becoming particularly close to Dandy, who, after two months, was herself still something of a newcomer.

It was hard to believe the quiet, and to Patrick's relief, there appeared to be no more donkeys in the area.

However, pasture was becoming a real problem. Dandy's owner offered his field, but its fencing proved too weak to withstand the ingenuity of Cherry and Pepsi, who arrived home before I did. I then tried tethering them in the long grass down the public footpath beside our house.

'Your mokes are disturbing my bees,' said Sid Green, 'they're going to get stung.'

Sid's bees were safely concealed on the other side of the hedgerow but one didn't argue with Sid.

I decided to investigate the Donkey Rescue Centre at Wormley and was met by the owner, the redoubtable Kay Lockwood, a Barbara Cartland look-alike. In her white stiletto boots and white fur coat she took me on tour of her seven hundred donkeys. There were plentiful clean stables, up-to-date hospital facilities, an army of farriers and a hay bill of £25,000 a year. What quickly became evident, though, was that although the donkeys had several acres of land to walk over, they were so numerous that there really wasn't room for mine. My donkeys' lot would not have been improved by going there, and I decided that for the moment Dandy and Pepsi should stay.

So grazing remained a problem, until one day a friendly telephone call unexpectedly came to our rescue.

'This is Mr Theobald here. You don't know me, but I'm a neighbour from up the road,' said the voice. 'Your pasture looks rather bare –' this was an understatement – 'I wondered if you would like the use of my six-acre paddock for your donkeys for the summer.' This was manna from heaven, but nothing in the donkey world is straightforward. If they went from threadbare fields to lush pasture they would immediately get severely ill from laminitis. Mr Bridger the farmer came to the rescue, volunteering to cut the field and bale the hay for me, but still there was potential danger, as six acres is a very large area.

'Why don't you invest in some electric fencing?' said Mr Theobald. 'Then they can safely graze in strips.'

Off I went to buy a mushroom-shaped battery, the best, I was informed, for our weather conditions, and yards of electric wire. We installed it, it worked, and the donkeys went on their summer holidays every year, under the watchful eye of good Mr Theobald. For the winter months they returned to the shelter of the stables and pigsties of Poplars Farm House and their luxurious diet of sweet-smelling hay and pony nuts.

Our one remaining problem was that the donkeys were now so happy together that they could not be separated. You did so at your peril; the noise would be deafening, Cherry Blossom and Pepsi would crash through reels of barbed wire and electric fencing in thirty seconds flat, and mayhem would ensue. Even the summer and winter exoduses up the road had to be organized with military precision so that they were all taken in one go. When we tried to take them in two groups poor Mr Theobald, who had just come from the hospital, followed on shortly after us shouting feebly 'Help, help' as the second group of donkeys came careering towards us.

With the pasture dilemma resolved it seemed that we were just going to have to get used to being a six-donkey family. At least Sid Green stopped complaining, and Cathy enjoyed her sleep once more.

Peace reigned in the paddock once more and Patrick was making good progress on his novel *The Wings of the Morning* about life in the Royal Flying Corps, based on his father's journals of the First World War. In the summer months he wrote in the cow-shed library surrounded by his books.

Much to Patrick's apprehension, I was fast friends with Min Flower and still visited her animal sanctuary regularly.

'Darling,' I said one day, 'Min has the most beautiful blue-eyed half Siamese, half Burmese cat – just like Kim – that needs a home.'

'No,' said Patrick, 'we've enough cats – and look at the last two, they were supposed to live in the barn, and already they're in the house.'

'What is more,' I continued, ignoring his comments, 'it's lived in a flat all its life and hardly wants to go outside, so that means it won't get run over.'

'No,' said Patrick.

It took six weeks of affectionate badgering to get Patrick to pay a visit to Min Flower's.

'He's so beautiful, he looks like a Rodin sculpture,' I coaxed, as the patrician blue-eyed grey cat purred at him. 'Also he can live in the library – you need a cat there. Cats are excellent companions for writers.'

This may well have been the turning point, as Patrick had recently found to his dismay some mice nesting amongst his first editions. There was a resigned sigh. 'Oh, very well,' he said gloomily, 'but this must be the *last one*.'

For a while all was well, Patrick named him Hodge, after Dr Johnson's celebrated pet, appropriate for a library cat, the idea being that he would sit on Patrick's desk and watch him as he worked. However, being of a superior intellectual intelligence, Hodge soon became no longer content to stay in the library but assumed the whole house as his territory. Bomb-proof Coley was both irked and fascinated by Hodge and would follow him about all day, day after day, driving him crazy. Finally, Hodge could stand it no longer and they came to blows not once, but several times, and the vet's bills for abscesses and septic wounds demanded that action be taken. The trouble was that some months had elapsed and we loved those two remarkable felines, 'Hodge the talking cat' and 'Coley the dog cat', equally, and could bear to part with neither. Fortunately, however, Hodge's previous history dictated an easy solution as he would only go out for half an hour at a time. We therefore locked Coley in for those thirty minutes and for the rest of the time Hodge enjoyed his indoor existence, with Coley outside, and the two of them spent many happy hours snarling and spitting at each other through the window.

For all the rewards of a talking cat though, it has to be said that there are some disadvantages, especially if it sleeps on the bed with you. One is that when it suffers a nightmare it can be a noisy one and you may suddenly be awoken by claws being embedded in your flesh. The main problem though is that such cats don't sympathize with lying in, or sleeping late, and insist on getting you up at whatever time they arbitrarily decide is breakfast time. After a while we decided that our early-morning call was getting progressively earlier and I determined to invest in a cat bowl with a timer. That meant you could place food in it and set it to the required time, when the lid would open promptly. For a while it seemed we had discovered the solution, but eventually Hodge tired of waiting for it and would fling it round the room, crash, bang, smash, in an attempt to get it open. Sometimes he would succeed, but more often than not he would simply wake us up and I would have to stagger downstairs bleary-eyed and open the container. We eventually gave that scheme up, having decided we preferred the vocal wake-up call. Meanwhile Coley was quietly asleep, curled up with the dogs in the kitchen, while Blackie, Rex and Abbie if not ratting in the barn were curled up on their electric blankets in the conservatory, by the boiler. Patrick always claimed it looked like a suburban housing estate for cats. Moggies, it has to be said, are a lot less noisy to live with. However, the birds, mice and rats much preferred Hodge, who spent so much time talking to them that by the time he pounced they had had ample chance to flee. To the best of my knowledge the only thing he ever succeeded in catching was a moth, and I presume that is because moths don't have ears!

Hodge was the last cat I had from Min as, much to everyone's dismay, at a certain point Min felt no longer emotionally able to cope with Cat Rescue and retired to live a rather reclusive life with her own animals. I sorely missed her in my life and particularly the stories of her eccentric animal-loving friends; cockerels and hens always seemed a fraction boring as indoor pets but there was a particular lady with a cockerel who roosted at the end of her bed. When her friends came to tea, it was especially partial to scones with Tiptree jam. Min's great friend, Daphne, kept a tortoise she called Mr A. Torts, whom she had at first mistaken for a pebble on Bosham beach, in her flat in Chichester. Every morning she woke him up with a shower from a flower spray and through the day he was given gourmet meals of almond blossom, lettuce, strawberries, dandelions and Birds Eye peas (his favourite). During the day he accompanied her to Waitrose in her shopping basket, to the Cathedral Cloisters for lunch where they strolled on the grass and in the evenings he was a frequent visitor to the opera and musicals – I was told his favourite was Gershwin's *Oh Kay* which Patrick produced at the theatre – keeping time by swaying his head to the music. He had to be the only tortoise in England with a personal passport, as Daphne refused to go abroad on holiday without him and as you cannot bring a foreign tortoise into the country, so Mr A. Torts travelled with his own British documents. In winter he even had a hot-water bottle under him so he wouldn't feel the cold. What a loss Min and her friends were to me.

9

Chip 'n' Dale

With the numbers of animals increasing I needed to work to help pay for their appetites. Apart from acting occasionally in Patrick's productions, there were family reasons that made acting away from home, or filming on location, difficult. Both our fathers became very ill, and my father died in January 1985, and Patrick's a month later. Patrick and I both felt very depressed after witnessing so much suffering. My mother had a particularly difficult time adjusting to my father's death after so many years of marriage. Winter that year was dispiriting and protracted. My mother alleviated her loneliness by more frequent visits, and on occasion I drove over to her spacious Victorian house by the sea to keep her company.

It was on one of those visits to Hove that I met some friends, who said they were looking for a home for two English-born chipmunks. They had one of their own called Rosie, who was an enchanting little thing, running loose most of the day, very tame and well-disposed to everyone.

'I'll have to think about it carefully because of the cats,' I said. 'Coley has decimated the squirrel population so a tame chipmunk wouldn't last long around the house.' A conversation with Jim King soon assured their future as he enthusiastically converted the old bull pen behind the farm into a large chipmunk-proof enclosure.

Soon they were installed in their quarters with all mod cons: running water, several cockatiel nest boxes, various kinds of branches to exercise on, and sleeping quarters made to resemble the hollow of a tree.

My young nephew, Mark, was staying with us at the time and was ecstatic at the prospect of real live TV characters arriving.

'You must call them Chip 'n' Dale,' he said, 'after the chipmunks in the cartoons.'

'Everyone in England must be calling their chipmunks Chip 'n' Dale,' I replied.

'But I don't *know* anyone else in England with chipmunks,' he insisted.

So Mark won the argument, and Chip 'n' Dale they became.

Visiting children adored the tiny creatures, maybe on account of their diminutive size, and would spend hours closeted with them stroking them, and feeding them by hand with grapes, strawberries, nuts, pumpkin and sunflower seeds, not to mention the odd maggot.

They certainly were the easiest creatures to look after; shrewdly, they used one nest box as their loo, another to sleep in, and the third to store food. Apart from cleaning them out once a month you didn't have to worry if you forgot to feed them. With the same hoarding instincts as squirrels, their food plate was always empty, because they had stored most of it away in their nesting box for a rainy day.

The chipmunks were well protected from the cats but did afford them a new pastime – watching chipmunk television. Frequently we found four cats at a time sitting in front of the wire netting with a bemused stare, watching the antics of the creatures within. And the chipmunks, supremely confident of their safety behind the tiny meshed wire, loved to torment them, doing backward flips and somersaults right in front of their noses, playing tag, or washing themselves, a paw's distance away. What exquisite torture, the cats would stay riveted for hours; and if ever they failed to respond when we called them, we knew where to find them. Transfixed by the bull pen – in front of the chipmunk television.

In 1986, Patrick produced the Gala *Fanfare for Elizabeth* for the Queen's sixtieth birthday at the Royal Opera House, with Steve Minchin who directed it for television. It was during this period that Steve asked me to compère the 'Miss United Kingdom' and 'Miss World' shows. It was a daunting prospect, the programmes went out live, and, unlike acting, you had to think on your feet quickly and coolly, and be your unruffled self. However, I hoped my fluency with Latin languages would prove useful and, with the South American girls, it did.

Once again Gladys and Jim King came to the rescue, and looked after the animals while I recorded the programmes in London and Hong Kong. In the event, the shows with my fellow presenter Peter Marshall were very successful, and it was rather a blow when Thames TV, bowing to pressure from women's lib, dropped the programmes in spite of high ratings – five hundred million people had watched them, all over the world.

Upon my return I was saddened to hear from the Kings that they would no longer be able to continue with us as they were moving to Chichester. They had managed to sell their cottage at a handsome profit and with the proceeds had bought a lovely house right in the city. I was very pleased for them, they were rather isolated out by Church Norton, and it meant that Gladys, who didn't drive, could get around Chichester by bicycle or on foot, instead of being stranded in the country. There is only one bus that passes through our village once a week, on Fridays. Jim was more reluctant to leave, but pronounced he would continue to help out on an occasional basis. This turned out to be more than he had bargained for.

I really was in a dilemma now. I badly needed someone to help me with the extended family of animals if I was going to be able to continue acting. Then, when I was looking at a farmhouse for a guest director – I sometimes helped find houses for visiting artists to the theatre – I noticed how it resembled our own. I remarked to the owner on her numerous horses, dogs and cats, and asked how she looked after them all.

'Oh, I couldn't cope alone,' she said, 'I have this wonderful lady, Jessie, who helps me, she adores the animals.'

Just the person *I* need, I thought enviously. 'I have lots of animals too, and I'm desperate for someone to help with them . . . you don't think, by any chance, she might have some free time, do you?'

There was a short pause. 'Jessie is in great demand locally, but you might just be lucky – I'll get you her phone number.'

'Mrs Howling?' I wasted no time in contacting her. 'I have been given your number, and wondered if you might have some spare time to help with my animals?'

'What are they?' she said.

'Oh, we have some ducks, hens, chipmunks, cats . . .' I faltered, 'and we have two dogs, very nice and sweet, they're dobermanns.'

She laughed. 'Oh don't worry about that – I've got two rottweilers and an alsatian!'

A few days later a commanding figure in a crash helmet straddling a diminutive moped turned into the drive, and into our lives entered Jessie. A tall, handsome woman with curly grey hair, she has natural authority and is instantly friendly with a generous warm smile. It

Goosey laying her first egg.

The duck pond at Poplars.

Frank Page with his champion Indian Runner.

Dennis Fenter at his bird hospital.

Kipling and Barnaby as puppies.

Sophie (*left*) and her adolescent son, Kipling.

Dorrit and Daisy in the dunes at East Head.

Patrick and me enjoying a quiet moment with the dogs.

Lady finding love with new owner Gordon.

Camilla the Chinchilla.

Sheba the Siamese.

Fanny One and Fanny Two!

Jessie and Jim, my stalwart friends.

(*Clockwise from top left*) Cardy, his friends Coco and Maisie, and Hodge the talking cat.

Phoebe, aged four (*left*), and Cherry Blossom the Escapologist.

Dandy (*left*) and Pepsi – the new arrivals.

soon became obvious that she was one of those people who can't sit down, she was always on the go. Previously she had only looked after cats and dogs, she said, but she was very willing to learn to deal with the Poplars Farm House residents, ferrets included. She was also, with her husband, John, perfectly happy to move in if we had to go away. Within a few days Jessie had taken over Gladys's and Jim's mantle with confidence and skill, and had all the animals very much under her control. It was a great relief to me to know they were in such good hands, animals responding just as human beings do, to natural assurance and confidence.

Jessie was more than delighted to look after everything when Patrick and I were invited to Windsor by Queen Elizabeth, the Queen Mother, to give a poetry reading one evening to her weekend guests. We were also warned that other members of the Royal Family often 'dropped by'. We decided to read from Jilly Cooper's charming anthology *The British in Love*, and set off to arrive as invited in time for tea. It is said that apparently most people dream, at some time or other in their lives, about the Royal Family, and in most of the dreams, the Queen Mother is pouring out cups of tea! At Royal Lodge, to find the Queen Mum actually pouring out the tea, and handing round the scones, was an extraordinary experience. I was also enchanted by the homeliness of the place with works of art on the walls, and Corgis' bean bags scattered around. Time to change into evening dress and then drinks, and at a signal the guests (the poet laureate, Ted Hughes, among them) retired to their chairs and we were left standing on a small stage area. Our composure was slightly shaken when we were joined by Princess Margaret and the Queen, who was sitting approximately four feet away. The poetry reading went very well, but the performance had a certain feeling of unreality about it, I think I would have been hard-pressed to conjure up such a dream. After our 'show' we then joined everybody for dinner, and thoroughly enjoyed the Royal Family relaxed at home, and informal. We were really performers, but made to feel like guests at a country house party. A sweet touch was that the Queen was tired after dinner, and wanted to go back to Windsor Castle, but wouldn't leave the dinner table before her mother, who was, as usual, having a wonderful time. Eventually the party disbanded and we drove back home overwhelmed by our remarkable evening.

Another unusual social occasion concerned the then Prime Minister, Margaret Thatcher. Peter Charlesworth, my agent, called me up at home and said: 'Ten Downing Street wants to know if you speak Italian.'

'Pull the other one,' I replied.

'No, no, it is quite true. They are having a dinner for President Fanfani of Italy, and all his ministers, and want to know if you speak Italian.'

'Yes, I do,' I said. 'Are they asking my husband as well?' Yes, they were, as it turned out, and we were both thrilled to be invited. I had, in fact, not spoken Italian for some time, but when you learn a language at the age of four it penetrates the brain cells so deeply that it never leaves you. I did, however, start to get the Italian newspaper *Corriere della Sera* to brush up my political knowledge.

On the night I found myself sitting between the Italian Minister for Defence on my right, and the Minister for Power on my left. Thanks to a large article about people demonstrating in the streets about the proposed nuclear power station near Pisa in *Corriere della Sera* I amazed the gentleman on my left with my knowledge of Italian affairs, and thanks to the same newspaper, I managed a reasonable conversation about the proposed co-production

Italian-English helicopters with the Defence Minister on my right. There were a lot of speeches but the most memorable moment was to occur after Mrs Thatcher made a short and precise welcoming speech.

President Fanfani rose to his feet and addressed the guests (who included Geoffrey Howe, Francis Pym and Michael Heseltine) for twenty minutes in Italian without giving the translator a chance to intervene. Finally, as he finished his long rhetorical monologue and the translator just opened her mouth to begin, Margaret Thatcher said: 'Well, I'm sure we all understood that wonderful speech, thank you very much.'

She had cleverly saved us from another twenty minutes of sheer boredom – it certainly showed her quality. Later as we came to say goodbye, Mrs Thatcher singled Patrick out. He was very flattered by her homework – she knew he ran the Chichester Festival Theatre, and told him (to his surprise) that her daughter Carol had worked in the restaurant there, whilst a student.

'Which only goes to show,' she said, 'what I keep saying. Even with all this unemployment, if someone really wants a job there is always a job to be found!' I think she was unaware how poorly paid the seasonal theatre restaurant waiters were. The jobs were fine for itinerant students, but would hardly have been sufficient for a married man with a family. It was another memorable evening, particularly of a formidable Prime Minister.

10

Daisy and Little Dorrit

The disadvantage of all animal husbandry is not only the massive and never-ending food bills but the vets' bills as well, and I often rued the day I hadn't become one. Some years have their fair share of disasters, but one particular black year my three beloved dogs all died within a few months of each other. The first casualty was Sophie who developed a small cough one day.

Her downfall had been her love of food once she was spayed, and we had been too indulgent with her, and, like Topsy, she growed and growed.

'She's too fat,' said Mr Vinnicombe, 'and the cough is indicative of a chronic heart problem. However, with pills we should be able to keep her going for a while.

'The first thing is she *has* to lose weight. No biscuits, no red meat, just turkey, chicken and fish and not too much of that,' he added.

In desperation I consulted my friend Oliver Graham-Jones and Mr Macleoud, the homoeopathic vet, but they concurred: there was nothing else to be done. She lost weight, but improved only temporarily. It was five months of walking a tightrope. Our clever vets had juggled Sophie's diuretics and heart pills until finally no combination had any effect. It was a Sunday, Patrick was away, and I had to call the emergency vet round to put her down and end the suffering. I had never had to put an animal to sleep before, so I accepted my friend Diana Carver's offer of help with alacrity. She had recently had to put her alsatian to sleep; so she rushed over.

Fortunately, as Sophie was terrified of male vets, the vet that day was a lady. She was so kind and really took the responsibility away from me by saying that if I didn't take the decision then Sophie was going to die slowly, in agony, over the next twenty-four hours. Diana collected a box of our favourite Belgian chocolates from the kitchen and we laid her on the bed which I had moved into the dining room, in order to be with her at night. She was so intent on eating the chocolates that she ignored the needle going in – I don't think she even noticed it – and quietly passed away in my arms. My mother later said she hoped I would do the same for her, one day!

Appallingly, however, as it turned out, I had to do the same for Ben, the white retriever, only a few months later. He had come to stay whilst my mother was on holiday and I noticed a peculiar bump on his head. Mr Vinnicombe said that even if they X-rayed they wouldn't be able to operate, whatever it was, so there seemed no point in doing so. Shortly afterwards, Ben had a nasty convulsion, but, as Mr Vinnicombe said it could be quite a while before the next, we proceeded as normal. It was only eight days before he had another, and I refused to go anywhere without him as he was always very frightened when he came out of it. On the ninth day, perhaps slightly prophetic, I took the dogs on Ben's favourite walk to East Head: this had been the very first walk we ever took him on without a lead, when he arrived at Poplars, aged only six months. East Head has a long sandy beach with sand dunes leading round to the yacht basin and views of the South Downs, Hayling Island, and the Isle of Wight in different directions. Ben, with Kipling, rushed in and out of the sea, and up and down the sand dunes like the puppy he used to be, his long tail wagging all the time. Because Sophie was dead and he had no occasion to be jealous, in all the time Ben stayed with us, Kipling was no longer aggressive towards him and they had a lot of fun. However, that same night, also a Sunday, Ben had a sudden terrifying fit which included turning somersaults, and when he came round five minutes later he could not stop whining, he was so terrified, and in distress.

Mr Vinnicombe arrived within fifteen minutes, and this time Patrick fed Ben chocolate biscuits as the injection went in; poor, sweet Ben just could not bear life any longer. It seems unjust that such an innocent animal should end up in such a horrible way, but then when is life straightforward?

We buried Ben next to Sophie, in a shadowy part of the garden beneath the poplar trees, and planted a rose bush on each grave. There was something very reassuring about their lying together in such a pastoral spot, alongside our white cat, and a few ducks, instead of sending their bodies casually off to the incinerator. My mother was distraught, but Ben had been very contented with us, and I was glad to have spared her his last terrible moments; had she witnessed them, the shock might well have killed her as well.

Hard as it was to lose Ben and Sophie, there was some consolation in still having Kipling with us. He was always so energetic and optimistic, the bean bags still had a purpose and our routines of waking and walking remained the same. However, we soon found that we had a problem, and that was Kipling himself; having lived with his mother for the six years of his life he could not function on his own. He had always followed her, imitated her, and been bossed about by her and he missed her terribly. He was miserable enough when we were with him but Jessie reported that whenever we were in London he would just curl up in a ball and refuse to eat. The only thing that would cheer him up was the arrival of a friend's Jack Russell bitch, who at least persuaded him to go out on walks. When I went away to do a theatre play for six weeks things went from bad to worse and we realized something had to be done, but what? The situation was not at all straightforward. Kipling was a sociable dog who was very protective of his own territory, and whilst totally devoted to humans, he had been known to savage any strange dogs that ventured into the house. It was therefore with some trepidation that I started to investigate the possibility of getting another. Mr Vinnicombe advised us it could only be a bitch puppy, and we thought the more like Sophie she was, the more likely Kipling would be to take to her. I rang the length and breadth of the country looking for such a creature.

First of all I rang Dobermann Rescue's branches in both Kent and Sussex in the hope that they might have a young bitch who was, say, the victim of a marriage break-up or repossession, as is so often the case these days. There was a six-month-old black male, or a two-and-a-half-year-old brown spayed bitch, but it was unlikely that Kipling would accept either of them. I was told of a litter in East Kent, but was advised by my friend, Jo Gibbs (the owner of Kipling's father and a dobermann judge), that they were German imports, and likely to be less placid in temperament. She then told me of a litter in Lincoln which belonged to an owner and breeder called Wendy Burge. Coincidentally, I had known Wendy when she lived in Chichester, and I knew hers were the friendliest of dogs: you could put your hand through her open car window with four dobermann bitches inside and withdraw it intact though somewhat wet with kisses. In the event, though, it was Jo who turned up trumps when she told me of a four-month-old brown bitch that a breeder had decided not to keep as she was emigrating to South Africa.

When I arrived at Di Patience's house in Croydon, two fierce dobermanns snarled at me through the door. Was this all a big mistake? I asked myself. But no, true to form, once I was ushered in by a petite blonde woman they turned into soppy lapdogs, or rather book-ends. The brown female called Daisy leant against my left leg, and Dylan, the black male, leant against the right one. I instantly fell in love with Daisy, the mother of the puppy, as she so resembled Sophie in every way, and in fact I actually said: 'Can I have her instead of the puppy?'

'No, you can't,' was the reply.

The puppy, at four months, was rather timid, and knew better than to vie for my attention with her two parents, who were monopolizing both my hands. However, I knew that in terms of size, she would be able to withstand Kipling much better than an eight-week-old tiny bundle. The deal was struck and I left with Di Patience's words ringing in my ears: 'I do warn you, she's rather intelligent.'

We obeyed her instructions to the letter. Initially, the puppy was separated for a few days from Kipling by a gate in the conservatory through which the two dogs could smell each other and get to know each other without incident. For their first walk I took them to the neutral territory of the beach at East Head, and with trepidation removed Kipling's muzzle and, although I was a nervous wreck watching, they played and romped together in and out of the waves. After that success I had enough courage to let them be together unmuzzled in both garden and house and all seemed to proceed smoothly enough. In fact, it quickly became clear that

Kipling adored the puppy; the puppy found that out too, and proceeded to walk all over him. She would push him out of his food bowl and climb on top of him in his bed, none of which worried him in the least, he was so besotted with her. They would play endlessly, but Kipling at six did not have the stamina of a young puppy and it was then that she would turn her attention to more damaging purposes and anything she could reach standing on her two back legs was fair game: my filofax, the telephone directory, the London *A to Z*, and much more, was frequently to be found in the form of confetti sprinkled liberally round the kitchen; we never knew when we came home what new disaster we would discover. She was, exactly as her owner had told us, extremely intelligent, and mastered anything including our dog fence very quickly. Kipling had lived happily confined within a four-foot fence he could easily have cleared for six years, as had Sophie and Ben, but in no time the brown puppy was over it, and twice a day would join our neighbours with their own dogs on walks. The only solution was a six-foot fence, all round the garden which, together with the fencing we require to keep in Cherry Blossom, really does make us impregnable.

Mysteriously, however, Kipling, at the height of his vigour, became unwell, either off his food or sick, and I had to take him to the vet.

'It's gastroenteritis,' said Mr Vinnicombe.

'Are you sure?' I replied. 'Where we walk we rarely see another dog, so it would be difficult to catch something.' The treatment didn't work, and within twenty-four hours I was back. This time the lady vet diagnosed an enlarged prostate and within twenty-four hours of treatment for that not succeeding I was back again. Uncharacteristically, Kipling stood hunched and tensed, and in pain. It was becoming obvious by now that things were really serious, but the blood tests could not get through to the laboratories because of that winter's ice and snow, so fate was not on our side. At the weekend I was desperate, Kipling was so unwell. And back I went. This time a temporary vet was on emergency duty. She gave the dog an intravenous drip, but as she left him alone in his cage all day, he pulled it out. The whole weekend was a nightmare. Monday he had to go on the drip again, and on the Tuesday, in desperation, Mr Vinnicombe decided to operate. Poor Kipling had a massive peritonitis.

'I could try and remove most of his colon, but he will be in great pain.'

Much as I wanted poor Kipling to live I loved him too much to want him to have a life of suffering – he'd always been vibrant with energy – so I made the difficult decision to ask them to put him to sleep on the operating table there and then. Sophie, Ben and Kipling had all died within seven months of each other. It was almost too much to bear, and Kipling, our glorious black-and-tan dog, was buried next to the other two in the garden under another rose bush.

This now left us with a destructive puppy, and no companion to exhaust her. Also, an unguarded house with a puppy, unable, as yet, to bark, in an area vulnerable to burglars. I began to have restless nights listening for strange sounds outside. It was also unfair to leave a young puppy for hours on her own, so I started to take her around with me. We christened her Little Dorrit because, as Patrick said, she was as immature as a Dickensian heroine.

'I think we had better get another dobermann,' Patrick proposed one morning. 'I don't like leaving the house unattended, except for a puppy and an alarm.' No sooner had he finished speaking than I was on the phone to Dobermann Rescue, this time in search of an older animal. I very much wanted a black male dog from Rescue, but when you take on a guard dog, you really need to research their character thoroughly as so many have been badly treated, and might become unpredictable. I was just deciding on a one-year-old 'Isabella' male (silver-beige in colour) when Di Patience, the original breeder of our little puppy, rang.

'You know I'm off to South Africa,' she said, 'well, it is too expensive to take both my dogs. Would you like Daisy, the mother of your puppy?' This was of course, the book-end bitch and Sophie look-alike I had so coveted when I went to pick up Little Dorrit, so I said 'yes' immediately. I tried to persuade Patrick that we should take the Isabella male as well, but to no avail! I did, however, hear that he went to a very good home with children whom he smothered in kisses, so all was well.

Poor Daisy – finding herself in a new home at the age of six (middle-aged in human terms) can't have been easy, and she had a lot of adjusting to do. First, she chased off the cats, but was an obedient dog and learnt that Coley and Hodge were allowed to be in the kitchen too. However, she did have a nasty habit of picking them off as they came through the cat flap, and the conservatory gate had to be restored to allow the cats to get safely back into the house; once they were in, she would leave them alone. She had also forgotten, as dogs do, that Dorrit was her daughter, and was particularly bossy at the start; but in time they really behaved like mother and daughter as they slept together, played together and walked together. On the whole, she really was a very good influence on her daughter as she was so well-behaved, but we soon discovered how true the old adage 'you can't teach an old dog new tricks' was. It took weeks of lessons for Daisy to master the dog flap which her daughter had conquered in one go and we finally achieved success only by putting her food the other side of it; Daisy was always so greedy she soon got the hang of it. As a town dog, she responded very differently from my London dobermann, Blue, to the country. Whereas Blue only wanted to play with his ball the whole time and ignored rustic smells, Daisy, at the age of six, discovered the thrill of the chase. This well-behaved dog reverted to the call of the wild with a mania that ignored any calls or whistles or threats from us whatsoever. Hares, pheasants, partridges and rabbits, all were her prey, and she would go missing for hours and never return home voluntarily. Fortunately, she wore her name tag, and some neighbour or other would frequently ring at eleven-thirty at night saying, 'I think we have your dog here.' The police were getting rather used to my frequent calls, even fed up with them: 'Oh, it's you, is it, Mrs Garland?' they would say. 'Lost your dog again?'

The last straw was when, unable to find a wild rabbit in the fields, she conveniently found a pet one in a neighbour's garden.

'Would you like me to buy you another one?' said Patrick to the father who was comforting his weeping children.

'Don't you dare,' he said. 'You've done me a favour. I have been waiting for this blasted rabbit to die for some time.'

But we felt very remorseful. In spite of our neighbour's relief at the demise of the pet rabbit, it was obvious that Daisy's extra walk activities had to be curtailed. Thank goodness for the invention of the extension lead as, except when on the beach, I was able to restrict her to her leash, while her perfectly behaved, leadless daughter, rushed happily about, but always returned to base on time.

Little Dorrit recently developed the most extra-ordinary habit. Nightly as we returned from the theatre we would invariably find a live hedgehog curled up with her in her bed, although I did find one trying to get out through the cat flap! As she was now reaching maturity I sometimes wondered if she was nesting: the hedgehog was the same size as a dobermann puppy so maybe she was just mothering it.

Fortunately the hedgehogs were the only things she ever caught outside, which was just as well as our bird population was increasing all the time, but at least birds can fly.

11

Residents in the Annexe

'How would you like some baby guinea-fowl?' said Bob
Clark our farrier-blacksmith as he whittled away at the
donkeys' hooves.

'I'm ashamed to say I've eaten one once, but apart
from that I haven't a clue what they look like or what
they do,' I said.

'Well,' Bob said, 'they're really very nice, we had one
for years. They look a bit like small turkeys and just sit
about in the trees. Make a bit of a noise though, so you
mustn't put them too near the neighbours.'

Sid and Cathy Green's patience was sorely tried with
the donkey paddock just under their bedroom window; I
would have to tread carefully not to antagonize them any
further.

'What do I do with them then? If they're too small the
cats will get them.'

'I suggest you get a large rabbit hutch and run,' said
Bob. 'You can raise them there until they are accustomed
to their new home and big enough to let loose. Then
they'll fly away and sit in the poplar trees, they'll be very
companionable, you'll see.'

I duly went off to Combes, the pet centre, to buy my
large rabbit hutch which I installed next to the barn and
the old wall on the east side, where it was protected from
the fierce south-west winds. I then went over to the

116

riding school at Apuldram where the fowls were kept. Their poor broody mother hen was forcibly removed and the four baby guinea-fowl were put in an aerated cardboard box. They were peculiar-looking creatures with their beautiful grey and white speckled feathers like a *haute-couture* cape around their plump round bodies, contrasting strongly with their tiny blue faces. The most accurate description of their heads would be that of a cross between a King's Road skinhead and a punk-rocker, with tufts of spiky hair protruding from bald scalps and pale painted faces.

For two months they stayed happily in their rabbit hutch sleeping, eating, growing, familiarizing themselves with their surroundings, tweeting contentedly and occasionally practising a spine-chilling series of screeches as staccato as machine-gun fire. They made excellent night-watchmen.

Finally, they were big enough to withstand the cats and the allotted day arrived. Patrick and I reluctantly opened the rabbit hutch door, rather sorry that they would no longer be in such proximity, but away in the trees. Slowly they looked out, walked out and circled around our ankles. Flying? Trees? It was suddenly like having four troublesome, affectionate Yorkshire terriers – they were obviously imprinted with humans and enjoyed nothing better than being around your feet. However, this posed another problem: they refused categorically to roost in the trees and would obviously be sitting ducks, or sitting guinea-fowl, as far as the foxes were concerned. Luckily our London builder friend had left us three steel-mesh shop-window burglar panels we had used on our flat when there was scaffolding up outside. We hastily constructed an enclosure with them and netted over the top.

It was then I realized how very stupid guinea-fowl are and had no doubt that the expression 'bird-brained' stemmed from them. Despite having the familiar rabbit hutch in the run in exactly the same position as before, persuading four no-brained guinea-fowl to enter it nightly proved a formidable task. Rounding up guinea-fowl (sometimes called the foul guineas) was particularly difficult as they would not run in straight lines, but twisted and turned and circled and looped around you until you became quite giddy. One night Jessie couldn't get one in, and the next day it was gone and on another night teeming with rain I couldn't drive one in either and the following morning it had disappeared. Mr Fox no doubt developed a taste for guinea-fowl.

We were down to two and stayed that way, I'm pleased to say for some while. We should have moved their by now smart aviary to another place to rest the ground, but would we dare? No, they at last went in at night easily, often even waiting, fluffing out their feathers and doing a little Indian dance to show their pleasure. To move these small-brained creatures would have invoked disaster.

When friends came to our house what did they fall in love with? Henry the donkey perhaps, the pretty Magpie ducks, handsome Dorrit the dobermann or Hodge the blue-eyed Tonkanese cat? No, it was always the foul guineas sitting on the boiler in the conservatory with the cats, chirping at them as they passed by and following them everywhere they went with such devotion.

Visiting the Locksacre Bird and Fish Centre with me one day, my niece suddenly spotted a solitary guinea-fowl. I always assumed our affectionate guinea-fowl were females and so enquired as to the sex of this lone bird. After a great deal of discussion (no one is ever certain) they pronounced it was a male and we took it home. There, a major combat ensued as one of ours made a full frontal assault, which was hotly defended by the newcomer. Feathers went flying everywhere and it took a fair amount of bravery on our part to enter the fray and separate the two fiends. What were we to do? We obviously now had two warring males and one female, as she had just looked passively on while her two suitors fought over her. A local farmer who had female guinea-fowl only came to the rescue and our delighted newcomer went on to a life of total ecstasy, or so we thought.

Almost from that moment everything changed, and the guinea-fowl became more feared than the dobermann. They still showed affection to Jessie and myself, but anyone else was in serious danger of being pecked. I saw Patrick running across the lawn in his dressing-gown in the early morning with them in hot pursuit, screeching as they went, and there was a moment when I thought our new postman was going to refuse to deliver the mail. The other postman had told him stories of the ferocious guinea-fowl and I had to explain that they couldn't really do much damage, there has never actually been a case in court of someone being pecked to death by guinea-fowl!

The guinea-fowl hen then sat on eggs, which explained the cock's protectiveness; he was so caring towards her it was most touching, and he obviously forgot she was his sister! However, my conviction that they were bird-brained remained. She sat on the eggs all through the day on the old duck's nest she appropriated by the barn and at five o'clock abandoned them to go into her aviary for the night. What a mother! At that rate the species would speedily die out, especially as the farmer who wanted the male guinea-fowl rang to say he was a she, a female after all. In which case, that would mean we had *two females* so it would have been pointless to sit on the unfertilized eggs anyway – maybe she wasn't so stupid after all!

If Min Flower had been a loss to me, she was an even bigger loss to the cat population. My new friend,

Monique Turk, was already taking in strays at her Cat and Rabbit Rescue Centre, but no one was finding anywhere for the Rex cats to go. I had found one a home with the bursar of the local hospice and such was the cat's personality that she said 'This isn't a cat, this is a person!' Another one I gave to a lady who had already had two from Min in the past, but a third, a little female, I just could not find a home for. At the time, my brother was rather ill and Patrick, seeing how worried I was, thought that giving me another problem, like a wild cat, might take my mind off things, and agreed she should stay. Poppy was tortoiseshell, marmalade, white and black with a corduroy coat and black markings around her eyes. She was lovely, but, having been in a cage for eighteen months, she found even Patrick's library the most terrifying place, and would just hide behind the books spitting and hissing. After a whole month of coaxing and gentle persuasion she gradually learnt to purr, and slowly became a normal cat. But there was a problem; she hated the other cats, which was surprising as she had shared her cattery with several others. She seemed to fight with all of them, except Blackie, whom she tolerated, but as she was of fragile build, inevitably came out of the spats the worst. Finally I discovered another clever invention, the magnetic cat door, which we installed in the library. This meant that if she wore a collar with a magnet around her neck, the door would admit her and lock behind her, leaving the others nonplussed on the other side. Eventually, however, she became so anti-social that she would hardly go outside, preferring to be alone in the library, rather like an eccentric literary recluse. However, as she had not successfully integrated with our cat society I was permanently on the look-out for a more suitable home for her. It wasn't that we didn't love her, we did, but I felt that she would be better off with a no-cat family. One day my friend Liz, Bob's wife, came in to help with the animals and burst into tears; her old cat had been run over six months previously and now her replacement kitten had just been run over as well.

'How would you like a cat that won't wander outside?' I asked.

'You mean Poppy . . .' Liz knew her already.

'She's terrified of the other cats, and won't venture beyond the library. She really deserves a better home than us, and if you don't encourage her I'm sure she'll be very happy just being indoors with the family,' I told her.

'Well, it could be the answer. I'll have to talk to Bob,' she replied.

Bob was slightly more sceptical, so we agreed there should be a two-week trial period. Six weeks later she was still there and a transformed cat, queen of her own domain at last. She slept on their bed, she talked, she played ping-pong and football with the children, Nathan and Claire, washed and curled up with the Jack Russell, and showed no sign of missing Poplars Farm House whatsoever.

After that, with Patrick away at his Chichester Festival Theatre office, I used the library as a sanctuary for the forty-odd cats I rescued and found homes for. Often I would be sorely tempted to keep them, as, unlike a donkey, a rescued cat or dog shows signs of gratitude and appreciation, and you and they cannot help but become attached. At first Patrick objected, but the library was kept in such pristine condition that he could not find fault with them, it was a great deal dustier and mousier when no cats were there.

While Poppy was still in residence we had our first actor to stay in the annexe in the person of Jeremy Brett. However, there was one problem with letting the flat – our tenants had to like the animals, and be liked by them! I had surreptitiously put a cat flap in the door between the library and the annexe flat, so the cats had access if they chose. Thus Poppy made the acquaintance of Jeremy, and developed quite a crush on him, just as I did when I saw his Hamlet! He was acting in *The Secret of Sherlock Holmes* at Chichester, but spent all his free time with the little cat. It was quite a love affair, he always asked after her, and was rather disappointed when I told him she had gone off to live elsewhere. With characteristic feline loyalty, Poppy – happily ensconced with Bob, Liz, their two children and the Jack Russell – never gave Jeremy another thought.

Helena Michell, actress daughter of Keith Michell, asked if she and her husband Simon could occupy the annexe while he wrote a screenplay for Paramount. They absolutely adored the animals, and vice-versa, and in some respects they ruined things for those who came after. If we were out they would ask the dogs over, and the dogs would lie down contentedly and watch them work and then would be taken for long walks through the fields. However, the main problem was the guinea-fowl. Helena and Simon would feed them all kinds of titbits from their front door. After that, the guinea-fowl resented any residents who wouldn't feed them and the larger bird would attack them without mercy. When Sir Peter Hall and his wife Nicki came to stay they were persecuted by the foul guineas, but when I explained about Helena and the titbits they too fed them bread-crumbs from the front door and soon became better, if wary, friends.

Keith Michell and his wife, Jenny, have stayed in our annexe on three different occasions and they very much participate in farm life. Keith has been known to call me at 1.30 in the morning to let me know the fox had just crossed the drive, and were the ducks safely locked up?

They were, and we were sound asleep, but I have never *gule* minded being woken up when it concerns the welfare of the animals.

Hodge the Tonkanese, who was supposed to be outside exercising in the daytime, always knew a good thing and while the Michells were in the annexe he was always to be found beside them, basking in the sunshine of the bay window.

On one occasion, when Keith was starring in the Chichester production of Shakespeare's *Henry VIII*, he very kindly invited me along to the last night party. The trouble was, when I turned up at the theatre fully made up, coiffed and wearing a black *décolleté* dress with high-heel shoes, Keith walked straight past me.

'Keith, it's me, Alexandra,' I said as I rushed after him.

'Goodness, so it is. You look so different, I'm afraid I didn't recognize you without your wellies on!'

I was not surprised, it had happened before. At Poplars I was usually bare-faced, wind-swept, mud-spattered and wearing green wellington boots. One day, attired in evening dress, I had spotted Geoffrey Hamber, one of our neighbours, in the terrace bar at the theatre on a Charity Gala Night. I went up to him and gave him a kiss on the cheek. He recoiled in horror at this brazen advance from a total stranger.

'It's me, Geoffrey, your next-door neighbour, Alexandra,' I protested.

'Oh, goodness gracious,' he said, 'I didn't recognize you without your waders!'

Melvyn Bragg and his wife, Cate, stayed several times during the run of *King Lear in New York* and thoroughly enjoyed the countryside and the inmates of Poplars Farm House, allowing Coley the cat to sleep on their bed each night. Once Melvyn brought Salman Rushdie, accompanied by six members of Special Branch, secretly, to the theatre. Patrick was rather concerned about such a large police presence (more than for various Royal visitors) but one of the bodyguards reassured him. 'Don't worry about us,' he said, 'we'll just melt into the background. You won't even know we are there . . .'

During the interval Patrick bumped into one of the actors, Tom Hollander.

'What's this with all the heavies?' Tom asked. 'Salman Rushdie here or something?'

However, it was Melvyn's children, Alice and Tom, who most enjoyed coming to Chichester and were thoroughly enchanted by all the animals, stroking the cats, playing with the chipmunks, being chased by the guinea-fowl and walking the dogs. The highlight of their stay was our visit to the Rare Breeds Show, held annually at the Weald and Downland Outdoor Museum. We watched the young handlers competition, which was always good for a laugh as you saw the youngsters trying to cope with recalcitrant goats and sheep. It was a difficult event to judge as some of the animals were well-behaved so their handlers had nothing to do, whereas others were pig-headed and the children really had an opportunity to show how masterful they could be. And frequently the rare breeds were larger and stronger than their diminutive masters.

Unfortunately, every year so far we have arrived late at the Rare Breeds Show and, although I make a bee line for the various exotic ducks and hens they have invariably been sold. Come to think of it, maybe that is why Patrick sees to it we always arrive too late – but then he's always late for everything . . . This particular year the ducks and hens had been sold, and the pigs were absent due to a swine disease, which was a shame as I have always wanted a Sandy Oxford which is the colour of a fox with dark spots. We looked at all the magnificent varieties of sheep and especially the Wensleydales with their long Rastafarian tresses, the huge Sussex long-horned cattle, which go back for centuries, and the many different goats. I could easily have taken home some Pygmy Goats, they are so pretty and tiny – so much easier to push about. Finally we wound up in the rabbit tent with Alice, Melvyn's daughter, who had set her heart on having one. As they were all off on holiday, however, Cate pointed out that it would be impractical and they escaped without one. Patrick, though, must have been touched by the sun that day as he announced that he was buying a Belgian Hare. The Belgian Hare was, it must be said, a beautiful russet colour with fur softer than velvet, so I didn't need much persuading. I had never wanted to own a rabbit, they always seemed fairly unrewarding pets, but the rabbit breeders soon convinced me that the Belgian Hare was of superior intelligence and a more sympathetic companion than a rabbit. I said that it wouldn't be fair to keep it in a mere rabbit hutch so Patrick agreed that another aviary could be built. We wanted two for company but as the breeder pointed out that two males would fight, two females would fight, and one of each sex would fight to the death 20 per cent of the time, we left with one.

I had always heard that guinea-pigs made very good companions for rabbits and rang up my friend Monique at Cat and Rabbit Rescue to see if she had a spare one. She said she had a choice of two males – I took the one that was more hare-coloured and wouldn't clash . . .

At first I thought it wouldn't work as the randy hare wouldn't leave the guinea-pig alone and all I could hear was squeaks (not always enthusiastic) from the guinea-pig. However, Monique was right and the novelty wore off – in fact some days the hare would find my right arm as attractive as the guinea-pig, which I suppose might have been considered a compliment. In the beautiful aviary (with a wire net bottom as well so they could not dig their way out), they seemed very content and from time to time we even saw the guinea-pig trying to make love to the hare so I guess they were both happy. The hare was a very clean animal, adopting a one-foot-square patch of grass as his very own loo, whereas the guinea-pig messed all over the place, and a lot of time was spent cleaning up after him. I noticed that the guinea-pig was always in the large rabbit hutch and the hare outside, so I installed a tiny hutch as well. The hare went into the tiny hutch and the guinea-pig stayed in the big one.

Patrick decided to call his hare Tiney after the seventeenth-century poet William Cowper's pet hare – Tiney is a traditional country name for a hare – and he spent more time with him than any of the other animals at Poplars.

We were under the illusion that we were in the possession of a hare, and it certainly looked like a hare. However, Frank Page, the elderly countryman whom I had met when buying the Silkies, enlightened us.

'There aren't no hares in captivity,' he said. 'They tried but the hares always went mad like and they would never breed or cross-breed, it was hopeless. What you have there,' he said, 'is a rabbit what looks like a hare and is placid of temperament. You don't have a hare, and you don't exactly have a rabbit, but something middling – more like – well, for want of a better description – a hare-rabbit.'

Kenneth Branagh and Emma Thompson came to stay while Kenneth was playing *Coriolanus* at Chichester. At that time there was a little lilac Rex-Siamese and a very nervous Abyssinian in the annexe library and Emma would invite them into the flat to play with her when she needed a rest from working on her film script of *Sense and Sensibility.* She said that she really would have liked to have taken them home to London but that with her and Kenneth's frantic work schedules it really wouldn't have been fair to own an animal.

Thanks to an advertisement I had put up at the vets', I was contacted by a couple whose cats had died of old age and who were looking for two replacements. When Mr and Mrs Cross arrived I took them over to the cowshed-library and explained the background of the two cats, that they had been kept in a cattery before coming to us. However, thanks to Emma Thompson's attention they were no longer terrified of humans, in fact the Rex-Siamese had become manically affectionate, and the Abyssinian would come near, although she still wouldn't let you touch her. Much to my surprise the Crosses said they would take both cats as the two were friends, adding bravely that the Abyssinian would be a challenge. She certainly was – the only way I could catch the fiend was with a fishing net, and it was a miracle I wasn't scratched to pieces. Mr Cross watched in astonishment and I thought he would change his mind, but he didn't. As always – and I've now homed about sixty cats – I felt sad to see them go as I had grown very fond of them but I knew that with Mr and Mrs Cross they would be well cared for and thoroughly spoiled, and so it was with delight I received this letter a month later telling me how the cats were progressing in their new home:

Dear Mrs Garland,

Just a very quick report on the cats.

On Friday the little rabbit escaped, and Pussy Willow streaked past like a bolt of gold lightning in hot pursuit. I screamed and dashed after them, in time to see the cat coming back round the corner being chased by the rabbit.

Saturday was another nerve-racking experience. No sign of any cats for breakfast. It was very unusual for little Pussy Willow not to be there. The day passed and there was no sighting of them. I felt sick with worry. I was sure that the little one must be trapped or injured.

At about 9.45 p.m. Graham spotted them from his bedroom window, they were about two or three back gardens away. He whistled and they both looked very surprised. They were tempted in and everyone breathed a sign of relief.

Sunday dawned and Pussy Willow was there, but no sign of the Nervous cat (the family were still blocking every attempt I made to find names for them). I thought I could hear a cat calling when I called them in for breakfast, and Peter went out to search for it, without success. I think he had the first inkling of what it is like to call for a cat with no name!

We had to go out for the day, and when we got back Michael and I determined to have one last search before it got dark. At the top of the next road we found a small group of neighbours clustered round a tree looking up into the leaves – it was our feline friend serenading at the pitch of her voice. We claimed her and someone offered a ladder. Michael went back to get Peter, who put on his climbing shoes and a thick sweater. As she might have been up there all night we thought that we had better get her down fairly promptly.

I told Peter how you had succeeded and he set off up the ladder. She did not appear to appreciate his good intentions and he feared that she might run further up the tree in her panic. He made a grab for the loose fur on the nape of her neck but she dug her claws into the bark of the tree and held on for dear life. He managed to prise her free, but she struggled violently and he started to lose his grip. As she was in danger of falling he grabbed the nearest available bit and she sank her teeth into his finger and held on.

Embraced in a life-and-death struggle they slowly descended to safety. Peter managed to hold her round the middle and put her on the ground but she attacked his shoe in fury, so he proceeded somehow to carry her into the house with her punching her paws furiously into the air.

We got in the house and after putting out some food and water we retired to nurse Peter's wounds. His finger by this time had ballooned up. We cleaned up the scratches and dressed them, then checked that his tetanus shots were up to date.

After that we made a cup of tea and planned strategies for future occasions as she does seem to make a habit of it. A sack seemed to be the best bet and a pair of leather gloves.

At bedtime we checked the cat and she appeared to have recovered from her experience. She has 'birdomania'! (Manic obsession with birds.)

I think she chases the birds up the tree, then looks down and her courage fails, although goodness knows, she has the equipment to get back down, and is incredibly strong.

Next morning I think the cat must have felt that Peter was the winner in that round, because she ate a hearty breakfast, and stayed contentedly near the house all day.

However, she refused to come in during the thunder and lightning storm, although Pussy Willow kept going out to get her. She was finally enticed in and Graham crept out in the rain to shut the kitchen door behind her. She then shot off round behind the washing machine, but changed her mind when it went into fast spin mode, and exploded through the kitchen door into her lair in the dining room.

This morning calm reigned, and here endeth the fourth week.

Yours,

Pat

When Kenneth and Emma vacated the annexe Peter Wood, who was to direct *She Stoops to Conquer* at Chichester, called to ask whether he could take it over. However, much to my delight I had just been asked by my old friend, Myra Frances, to star along with John Challis and Mark Sinden in the three-hander play, *Dangerous Obsession* at The Mill at Sonning. This meant I would be away rehearsing and performing for eight weeks, and would stay at our London flat during the week. I therefore passed my landlady's hat on to Jessie, who said she was quite prepared to look after the animals, as well as Patrick and Peter, so I was free to accept. It was just what I needed to raise my self-esteem and spirits. However, when you act infrequently you are at a disadvantage compared with actors who go from job to job and it was hard work learning such a large part.

Thanks to Myra Frances, our director, *Dangerous Obsession* proved a huge success with the public, playing to capacity every night. The Mill Theatre, at Sonning-on-Thames, near Reading, was a joy to work in. Privately owned, and very well organized, it is situated right on the river. The seating capacity of the theatre is limited, but the owners had cleverly linked it to the restaurant overlooking the water so they were able to provide a dinner-theatre ticket for a reasonable price. This proved to be a unique experience as we actors would get ready ahead of time in order to have dinner with our invited guests beforehand. At 8 p.m. there would be the announcement: 'Ladies and gentlemen, will you please take your seats as the performance will begin in five minutes', at which point we would excuse ourselves from the table, dash backstage, change and step on stage uttering the first line on cue two minutes later. Often during the run-up to the start of a play one gets very nervous, but at The Mill there was no time for any of that – it was far too social!

All too soon the play was over and it was back to Chichester and the relentless summer season there.

On the animal front, Dennis Fenter rang to ask if I would like a baby Canada goose in two weeks' time. I of course said 'Yes!' And, sadly for us but not for him, Mr Theobald rang to say he had managed to sell his house and six acres, so regretfully the donkeys would have to move on at the end of the summer. It was a problem, but fortunately not an immediate one as Mr Bridger, the local farmer, had piled hay and straw high up in the barn, so at least they would have a comfortable winter.

I was pleased, upon my return, that Peter Wood was still in residence. Peter, his cat, Tobermory, and parrot, Sid, were our favourite annexe guests. We adored having them and they loved coming, especially when Tobermory got the hang of things. Peter would arrive with his car bursting at the seams, as, apart from his own luggage, it also had to contain Sid the parrot in his cage, and Tobermory the white Chinchilla Persian cat. Sid's cage was positioned in the bay window of the sitting room where he would squawk at the guinea-fowl, ducks, geese and hens outside, and Tobermory had the run of the flat and the great outdoors. Tobermory, or Toby as he was sometimes called, by virtue of his long, and fluffed-up hair, looked a great deal larger than he really was. As a result all the resident cats were intimidated by his apparent vast bulk and wisely let him be. The exception was Hodge, the boss-cat, who screamed in outrage, and attacked whenever he saw the stranger. Hodge, who by now had got used to being outdoors, was out from 9 a.m. to 4 p.m. every day while his enemy Coley, the other top-cat, was shut in; thus Tobermory decided of his own accord that he would rather not go outside until 4 p.m. and certainly wanted to be let in by 8.30 a.m. If Peter was away at the theatre working, when Toby heard me call Hodge inside, and saw Coley emerge, he would scratch at his glass front door until I came to let him out.

One night when I was in the bath I heard terrible caterwauling outside, and feared for a moment that Hodge had managed to get out. I grabbed a bath towel and dashed outside only to meet Peter, also dripping wet in his bath towel, who had similarly come to the rescue. Fortunately, none of my cats were the culprits, it was the marauding black tom cat that looked like my cat Blackie. Somehow, clever Tobermory knew he shouldn't have been there and let him have it in no uncertain terms. I don't think that tom put in another appearance for the entire duration of Peter Wood's stay.

At first, Sid, the African Grey parrot, was intimidating and I had been warned that if he didn't like you he could use his beak to devastating effect. However, when Peter had late rehearsals it was necessary to check up on him, and slowly, slowly we became friends. Peter had never intended to have a parrot, but had needed one for his production of Congreve's *Love for Love* at the National Theatre. Sid played Ben, the sailor's parrot, but highly irritated Tim Curry, with whom he had most of his scenes, as he would frequently improvise and say 'Hello,

hello' in the middle of Tom's most important speeches, thereby bringing the house down. Tim was not amused, Sid got as many laughs as he did and a huge round of applause when he took his bow at the end. When the play finished someone had to have Sid, and Peter Wood ended up taking him home. They became inseparable and the parrot responded only to him. Sid had a large vocabulary and always used the right words at the right moment. Peter and I would have a debate as I would attribute reason to the parrot as Sid always said the appropriate thing for the occasion. Peter was of the opinion that he had a body clock which knew what was right at a particular hour of the day.

First thing in the morning when he heard Peter stir, he would say, 'Hello, Peter, good morning, want a cup of tea?' All day long he would imitate the telephone and the receiver being picked up, and a typical conversation in Peter's precise voice would be: 'Hello, oh huh, huh, yes, yes, right.' Then he would yell: 'Peter coming.'

At four in the afternon it was once again the clinking of cups and 'Want a cup of tea?' and then at 6 p.m. there would be the festive sound of corks popping, and wine being poured. Once we thought Peter was throwing a drinks party without us, but it was just Sid having a party on his own, pouring out the wine and acting all the parts. His cruellest joke was on the cat. He loved nothing better than to call: 'Tobermory, Toby' in Peter's voice until the cat would come rushing in thinking Peter was home, only to find a laughing parrot. However, let out of his cage with Peter he was the sweetest, most affectionate of birds, travelling around on Peter's shoulder and nibbling his ears. In the mornings he used to sit on the tub while Peter had his bath. Peter entered into the spirit of Poplars Farm House with its odd animal family, coming for long walks on the beach with the dogs and kindly letting out the ducks and hens as he was an early riser. But he resolutely refused to let out the guinea-fowl, and once asked Jessie, 'Why does a nice girl like Alexandra keep such foul birds?'

12

To Fly or Not to Fly and Militant Mokes

Even Peter was excited at the prospect of a human-imprinted Canada gosling, and at the due time I went off to see Dennis at the Bird Hospital.

In the meantime, the spacious hen aviary had been divided into two. The Silkies would have to share lodgings with the goose. When I went round to collect it, Dennis offered me another two human-imprinted goslings, and, being unable to say no, I went home with those too.

'Three geese,' said Patrick. 'I thought you said only one.'

'I did say one, but Dennis Fenter gave me three, what was I to do?'

Patrick conceded defeat, and was soon entranced by them, as indeed were all the adults and children who met them. They would follow you everywhere, pull your clothes to get your attention and gently nibble your fingers. When workmen were around they would keep them company all day and pick up each tool in turn as though to examine it. When we'd been out, on our return they would rush to greet the car with wings outstretched, giving shrieks of welcome and waggling their heads; they really seemed relieved that we were home and would follow us to the front door. That, to their sorrow, had to be shut until they were put to bed on the straw in their own aviary or you would find them by the boiler with the cats and guinea-fowl, and as they were not house-trained they would make quite a mess. However, Peter Wood didn't seem to mind and they would often follow him through his open front door into the kitchen where he would give them bread and tickle the backs of their necks.

Slowly the down disappeared to be replaced by feathers and their wings grew stronger. In the mornings they would be so excited they would take off and go once round the pond before landing on it and remaining earth-bound for the rest of the day.

I was, however, always aware that these pets were really wild birds and that there was no guarantee that they would stay with us. Peter said they had such a cushy life they would never leave, and we certainly hoped so, although I always worried that they would be bored and might go in search of people if no one was around.

The season moved forward – spring changed to summer. The fig tree outside the annexe burst into leaf. In due course Peter and his eccentric entourage left. It was a blow to see them depart as we had all become so fond of them.

Jean Boht, the actress, moved in as they moved out. Jean had come to Chichester to play Jessie in *Venus Observed* by Christopher Fry (in which I played Hilda) and Mrs Hardcastle in *She Stoops to Conquer*. We shared a large dressing room at the theatre and, both Pisceans, got on famously – she didn't even complain when one day two rescued cats were delivered to our dressing room at the matinée, to wait there until Kerry, our dresser, could take them to their new home that night.

One morning when we were called late to rehearsals we were sitting enjoying a nice cup of coffee in the conservatory with the dogs, watching the mass of different birds in the crab apple tree opposite. Suddenly Jean said severely: 'Your dog has fleas,' as she picked one off Dorrit, the younger dobermann.

'She can't have,' said I. 'I gave them both a dose of flea spray only two days ago.' At that moment my eye was caught by the vacant dog basket in which, to my horror, the bean bag was slowly heaving up and down.

'Oh my God, it's a rat,' said Jean, easing out of her chair.

'No,' I said, 'it's a hedgehog.' With that I lifted the bean bag and the little spiky animal was revealed.

'This is about the fourteenth hedgehog Dorrit has brought in this year,' I observed, as I went to fetch the pair of 'hedgehogs only'-designated oven gloves. I picked up the little thing and went and put it in the part of the garden unoccupied by the dogs, along with its thirteen friends.

Patrick swears it is the same hedgehog, which keeps on coming back, I just think it is amazing that Dorrit keeps on finding so many hedgehogs and can pick them up in her mouth without doing herself or the hedgehog any harm.

Jean would often help Jessie and me round up the animals before going to perform at the theatre in the evening, she particularly enjoyed the geese and, like many others, deeply disliked the guinea-fowl.

'I don't know why you keep them,' she said. Jessie agreed: 'Those guinea-fowl should go in the pot,' she said, knowing full well that would never be the fate of an animal or bird of mine. 'Look at poor Bob, he's having to work with a stick in his hand.'

It was true, poor Bob, the gardener, had taken to working with a long cane in one hand to fend off the larger guinea-fowl which would charge him from time to time when his back was turned.

'I'll put them in early,' I offered, 'if you can't cope.'

'No, they're all right,' Bob replied resignedly.

Funny that they never go for me or Jessie, but then I suppose they don't peck the hand that feeds them . . .

Venus Observed, which starred Donald Sinden as the Duke of Altair, was very well received at Chichester, but it was not without its dramas. Donald Sinden trapped his sciatic nerve, which caused him intense pain, and he was rushed off to hospital for major surgery. Michael Gee Jones, his understudy, replaced him overnight and did a magnificent job. However, Donald as the Duke of Altair was so very special, he would bring tears to the eyes every night as we watched his last speech about old age from the wings, so some of the magic had already left us. Then I received a blow – when I got back to the dressing room after the performance on the last night there was a message from Jessie to say that the Canada geese had flown. This was a true sadness, my little friends had gone, there was always another play.

Jessie had been the one who found them missing but, amazingly, when she checked later, the little greylag had come back. However, the other two geese never did and I worried terribly for their welfare. A week later when I was talking to the farmer across the road and trying to persuade him to take on one of my rescued cats I found out what had happened.

They had taken off from our pond judging their flight to clear the hedges and had landed bang in the middle of a huge greenhouse that was being erected on the other side of the road. All three geese were shocked, one flew back, one flew off and one ran away. If only I had known I would have gone off in pursuit. A few days later Jean swore that at 7 a.m. she saw one of the missing geese back at the pond drinking water, but by the time I got up to let out the rest, there was no sign of it.

I was distraught, I didn't believe my imprinted geese

were fit to face the cruel outside world. They loved people to the point of obsession, how would they know there were men with guns who would want to shoot them, and foxes that would want to eat them?

I rang Dennis Fenter: 'Do you think you could possibly pinion the wings of my little greylag goose, the two Canada geese have disappeared and I really am worried about them . . .'

'I wouldn't be too concerned,' said Dennis, 'besides I have another two baby Canada geese here, would you like them too? Just come and collect them.'

Karen, the stage manager of *She Stoops to Conquer* had asked me for the loan of a Silkie as Mrs Hardcastle's pet hen. I had to drop my white Silkie round at the theatre for a performance, so on my way back I called in at the Bird Hospital to pick up the two baby geese. They seemed even younger than the previous ones and were just as entrancing, hiding behind my skirts as though I was their mother. Typically, the greylag immediately took against them and wouldn't let them in her aviary so they had to be locked in a duck coop at night for a few days until the greylag got to know them a bit better and decided to be nice to them after all. They certainly were much better company for her than the ducks, and I was aware that as they were so young and downy they would not be trying to fly off for a while, and she was unlikely to go it alone. However, as time elapsed they grew in confidence, the soft fuzz was replaced by feathers and they started to test their wings around the pond, as had their predecessors. I was never worried about them when there were people around as they would spend the day most contentedly following them, but I started to worry when no one was about and they saw the wild mallards flying in and out, that they too would fly away. I did have a wild mallard, however, who had chosen to become tame like my domestic ducks and I hoped that the wild geese might do likewise.

One day as I turned into the drive my fears were realized. One of the Canada geese ran towards the car desperately waggling its head up and down and screeching and hooting dementedly. 'They've gone, they've left me.' It was obvious what it was trying to say and it seemed terribly relieved that at least I had come home. Immediately I went to find Cameron, the farmer across the road on whose land the earlier geese had alighted the last time, but he had not seen them. I went from field to field calling 'Goosey, Goosey', my unoriginal name for the greylag, and much to my surprise she flew back to our pond, but of the third there was no sign. An hour later the farmer arrived with a Canada goose under his arm.

'It was looking rather lost in a field, so I've brought it back,' he said.

I was so relieved, but what was I to do? Clearly this would happen again. Once more I rang Dennis Fenter and explained what had happened and the following morning I bundled two of the by now rather hefty geese into the boot of my car. He cut five of the flight feathers (it doesn't hurt them as it is like cutting a nail), and, having observed the procedure carefully, I came back and did the same to the remaining goose while Patrick held its wings.

Eventually the feathers will grow back and I will have the same dilemma all over again, and it is a problem: do you clip their wings and know that they are safe or do you let them join the dangerous outside world? I think this year as they have probably missed the flight to Canada I shall have to continue to pinion them, but maybe next year when there are more wild goslings needing sanctuary I shall let them go. I had no idea it was possible to fall in love with a goose.

*

Patrick's role as theatrical director and writer and mine as actress meant that virtually every weekend during the summer we would be invited to some charity event. My particular charities are the Brent Lodge Wild Bird Hospital, the local hospice, St Wilfrid's, St Richard's, the local hospital, and the NSPCC. One advantage of being married to the Artistic Director of the Chichester Festival Theatre was that I was able to persuade the theatre to give a performance of *The Merchant of Venice* in aid of the NSPCC in the presence of Princess Margaret. A great deal of work was involved organizing it and selling all the tickets at higher prices, but it was worth it, the evening was a huge success and made a lot of money for the charity. In fact our little branch raised over £70,000 that year.

On another occasion I had what I thought was a brilliant idea: for one race at Goodwood the champion jockeys would ride donkeys instead of horses. I thought it would be extremely funny as donkeys are so unpredictable. The jockeys entered into the spirit of it and volunteered their services immediately. The proceeds were to go towards a new scanner at St Richard's Hospital, something that apart from the obvious advantages for the general public, the jockeys would benefit from if they ever had an accident. Unfortunately the steward at Goodwood could only offer me a late race which was no use, as the jockeys would already have been flying in their helicopters on their way to another meeting. However, Isadore Kerman, of the Fontwell Racecourse, heard of our plight and offered us a day's racing with permission to keep all the sponsorship I could raise on all the races for the hospital. In any attempt at fund-raising you certainly find out who your friends are, and Mrs Henny Gestetner, my special friend on the Theatre Board, gave a large donation, along with

Mack's of Chichester and several others. I also organized stars to present the cups after each race and Gerard Glaister, the BBC producer, very kindly asked Jan Howard, who was filming *Howard's Way* along the coast, to come along and we had all the star actors from the theatre who didn't have a matinée that day.

The day was glorious and a splendid time was had by the punters, the stars and sponsors, and even the book-makers, as Fontwell put out the red carpet and entertained us royally. Best of all, a large sum of money was raised for the scanner at St Richard's. The only sad-ness was that we didn't get to use the donkeys after all as there was not enough time to obtain the inoculations necessary for them to appear on the race track. I still think it was a good idea, maybe another year!

After *Venus Observed*, all the charity weekends and the exhausting summer season, we decided to seek the tran-quillity of our Corsican retreat. Asleep in our mountain-top eyrie and hearing the donkeys calling to each other across the valley, at first I had nightmares about Sid Green and his shotgun and imagined my don-keys at Poplars escaping, which would slowly die away, as village sounds replaced them.

We had managed to take our two weeks' holiday at the end of the summer season. In fact being as tired as we were it was just the right amount of time. If you went for longer you were sucked into village life, sometimes at your peril! In August the population swells to five hun-dred in the little village but the basic voting population is more like forty-five, most of them related. So family loyalties are close-knit and intense. That year the village mayoral elections had been held with eleven candidates standing for office out of the forty-five residents, and as a result hardly anybody was talking to anybody! During our fortnight we therefore had to steer a very careful path through a minefield of village relationships, in an attempt not to offend anyone. On a sadder note, Ariane, our great friend, persuaded us to look after an alsatian bitch that had been abandoned by tourists whilst she found it a home. The dog had been living in a cave in the village and had been so maltreated by children throwing stones that she was terrified of them. Over the holiday I became terribly attached to her, but with our quarantine laws, it really seemed too cruel to bring her home to months of incarceration, and a restaurant owner said he would have her. I was distraught to learn later that she had been shot by them when she did no more than growl at a child.

There were so many animals abandoned on the island when the tourists left in September that wherever we went I would carry dog or cat biscuits in my handbag for the first starving face we came across. Sabrina, my neighbour's eight-year-old daughter, and I found one such creature, a tiny black kitten, sitting woefully bedraggled in the rain by the village dustbins. We followed it to its refuge alone in a cave and daily I went to give it food for the duration of the holiday. As with the German Shepherd, with our quarantine laws, there wasn't much I could do beyond feeding it, but I did manage to leave a large carton of dry food and lots of water for it when I left. Ariane fed all the stray cats in the village (which were numerous) and I knew if only the little feline would get strong enough, it would find her. She said later that a little black cat answering his description had turned up at her door and was doing well – I can only hope it was him.

It hadn't been the ideal holiday because of the weather either, as the Corsican summer season had ended and the torrential rain and violent electrical storms of October had been rather confining. We resolved another year to go somewhere warmer, further south.

Back at Poplars Farm with the central heating and cosseted animals all was well and capable Jessie had nothing troublesome to report except that there had been some phone calls about cats. There was also another letter from Pat Cross:

Dear Mrs Garland,

Just a short up-date on the cats, because I know you like to follow their progress.

Sadly, we recently lost both our rabbits as a result of a virulent virus. We were all devastated, and I think the cats missed them as well. They had all become best of friends, and although I had no proof, I had a strong suspicion that they aided and abetted Clover Clump when she periodically led a 'break out' and rampaged round the house.

We still have to stay vigilant when food is around, as the Si-Rex goes into a food frenzy and is found wolfing into packets of cheese or distributing slices of bread all round the kitchen. She is now growing a fine hair. Unkind people say that she looks like a skinny tatty rug, but we think she is lovely and are very proud of her hair! She has a problem trying to sit on everyone's knee at once as she doesn't want anyone to feel left out. At this moment in time they are both curled up together among my dirty washing! After I spent a fortune on a fur sling which hangs over the radiator, because she always has cold feet, ears and tail. She is the mistress of the impossible leaps which do not always succeed. I have never met a cat that thought it could walk along the top of sauce bottles until now.

On the other hand 'Nervous' was a terrible mis-
nomer for a cat. Selective, Canny Anny, Clumsy
Clot, would all have suited her better. She likes to
lie stretched out over three people of an evening.
She has moods when she wants to be tickled, and
will roll over at inopportune moments, forgetting
where she is (on top of the fridge) and fall off. She
is a champion smasher of objects, preferring not to
travel on a higher level than the floor. She is still not
too keen on being picked up.

I hope this news puts your mind at rest.

Yours,

    Pat Cross

As my cat-transit library was empty I felt able to
respond to the calls about cats and took on Camilla, an
extremely pretty, grey Rex-Chinchilla, and her daughter.
Camilla had been used exclusively for breeding until the
age of eight and had been in a cattery all her life. She
positively luxuriated in her new existence and loved
nothing better than to run from one end of the annexe to
the other, a distance she had never before been able to
cover, and she played manically with her toys like a
deprived child. Worse than her was her daughter, whom I
called Libra as she was still hiding behind the books after
six weeks. I could cuddle her on the top shelf and she ran
around the beams over a much larger area than her cattery, but she rarely had the courage to venture on to the
ground floor except when she had to eat or use the cat-
litter tray. The third member was, for the first time, from
a different source. Monique, my friend at the local Cat
Rescue, told me she had a two-year-old Siamese female
which had lived in a flat with several dogs. Sheba was
very nervous and had constant tummy troubles. I volunteered to take her on and try and sort them out. Six

weeks later she was much calmer and her stomach problems seemed to be cured. Like Hodge, the half-Siamese, Sheba was a talking cat with a calculating disposition, queening it over the other two cats; fortunately, being a female, she lacked some of Hodge's less appealing signs of displeasure!

Of superior intelligence, Hodge was prone to vent his irritation against the other cats and indeed us, in all manner of non-charming ways. Such was his character, though, that we adored him and tolerated his occasional peccadillos. However, on one occasion he did stretch Jessie's patience to the limits. The trouble was he liked everything to be in its place, and one day Jessie left her crash helmet on the boiler where he liked to sit instead of hanging it up as she usually did. When she came to put it on to go home, she couldn't wear it. The next day when she arrived on her moped she had it on.

'How is the crash helmet?' I asked.

'Since Hodge peed in it there are no flies on me,' she replied. 'Even Fairy Liquid and disinfectant won't get rid of it.' Jessie is such a good sport and very much an ally as far as the animals are concerned. She had to be, Patrick would have divorced me long ago if he had known half the things my animals had done to his precious books . . .

On another occasion, while Jean Boht was occupying the annexe, she and I were outside and saw Hodge looking out of the bathroom window at the four assembled cats stretched out in the sunshine below. Suddenly he pointed his rear end towards the open window and sprayed so that the drops fell on the dormant felines beneath. They shot up in disbelief at such a rude interruption, and a satisfied Hodge withdrew smirking into the inner sanctum.

Because of Libra's reclusive disposition Patrick thought there were only two cats in his library, Sheba the

Siamese, and Camilla. However, one day he came back clutching a book and looking rather surprised. 'Camilla spat at me from the beam,' he said.

I finally decided to come clean and admitted that there was a third cat there: the very nervous Rex-Chinchilla daughter of Camilla and that she had been there for six weeks. He thought about it for a moment.

'I suppose I can't complain about a cat that is invisible,' he said.

All three cats were very appealing in different ways, and as they were causing no trouble, I was delighted when one day Patrick weakened and suggested that they stay.

Often I was able to home cats directly without them coming to Poplars, so my animal rescue could still continue without creating too much domestic disturbance. In fact as Patrick was so busy with the theatre he was often surprised when we would get Christmas cards signed by ET and Radar or Bentley and Nelson.

'Who on earth are they?' he would ask with a perplexed frown.

'Oh, just cats,' I would answer.

My great horticultural passion is orchids, mainly because they occupy so little of one's time with watering. Each May all twenty-five plants are put outside and forgotten about until the following September. As a result, from Christmas onwards for two months our conservatory is a wonderful display of orchid spikes.

However, the high point of our Christmas season every year belonged to Henry, our first and original donkey, whose fame had spread far and wide. For Christmas Day he was always booked months in advance to appear as the humble ass in the nativity play at our local church, while Frances and Phoebe went on a Christmas pub crawl to raise money for handicapped children.

One Christmas Day was particularly wet and windy, but in our tracksuits we were able to give Henry a quick brush before the horse-box picked him up at 9.30 a.m. Patrick and I then dashed inside to change and I put on my new bright pink Mondi suit. We arrived at the church at two minutes to ten just before the procession of Mary and Joseph, wise men and shepherds started up the aisle. Henry brought up the rear with the largest shepherd and as he walked along you could hear the children whispering, 'There's Henry'; for them, each year, he was the star of the show, the service would not have been the same without him.

However, on this occasion as he processed along he stopped dead in his tracks and refused to budge. One of the shepherds, an angel and Joseph all went to the rescue, tugging at his halter to no avail. Finally, I could hold back no longer. I knew from experience that pulling was no good, and I put my shoulder under his bottom and heaved until Henry deigned to continue down the aisle. When I returned to my seat Patrick, grinning, pointed at my pink designer suit, Henry had been waiting in the rain outside and I was covered from head to toe in mud.

The vicar's sermon was also livened up as the youngest shepherd in the pageant was intent on hooking down the candelabra over his head with his crook. Disaster was averted as the priest finished his sermon in the nick of time and moved them over to the crèche where all the children from the congregation were invited to offer their gifts.

However, throughout the proceedings we were riveted by Henry's tail which was flicking ominously from side to side. Suddenly it went up, the children took a step backwards, and there was a tense silence as even the vicar paused in his address.

'I rather think Henry is about to make his offering,' he said, but slowly, slowly, Henry lowered his tail again.

Mercifully, it was a false alarm and the Nativity Play passed off successfully for another year. Henry seems to be miraculously house-trained, he has never let us down – yet.

After the loss of Mr Theobald's field, the donkeys had been posing something of a problem as their pasture was threadbare, and I was having to supplement their diet with my store of hay.

I had kept in touch with Mrs Carpenter, the previous owner of Poplars. She had just moved into Norton Priory, the luxurious nursing home nearby and shortly after her arrival she called.

'I was talking to the owner of Norton Priory,' she said, 'about your donkeys' lack of grazing and as they have thirty acres here next to Church Norton he has volunteered to have them for the summer.'

I accepted the amiable Roy Lewenden's offer of new pasture with alacrity and, transported by a friend's horse-box, the donkeys eagerly entered their new field. Everything was fine while they were strip-grazing, confined by the electric wire, and they revelled in all the gifts of carrots, apples and bread which were brought to them daily by the residents of the Norton Priory Nursing Home.

However, when they had the run of the entire field of ten acres full of lush grass the trouble started. The grass was always greener on the other side and Roy started to get reports of escapees in his neighbour's gardens. He remained good-natured about his mischievous charges, however, and kept on calling in his handyman with new poles and yards and yards of barbed wire. I didn't like to tell him that our paddocks looked like Wormwood Scrubs, although I did take him over the bicycle chain for the main gate!

They were also introduced to a new farrier, Peter Fenton, who claimed that donkeys were reincarnated farriers, they were so cantankerous. Dandy was the only one of the six mokes that played up, however, and I was instructed to cross her ears over and hold them flat against her head, thereby diverting her attention, and despite the odd kick Peter always succeeded in his work. The trouble was that Dandy had rarely had her feet done before she came to us, and you really need to get them used to the farrier at an early age.

The donkeys' fame continued to grow throughout West Sussex until demands for their services at various charity events became so numerous that I had to start limiting their appearances. A particularly memorable occasion was a fête at Runcton Mill for the local Hospice, when we decided to risk taking all six so the noise of the ones left behind wouldn't deafen our neighbours. Gillian Plowman, the bursar of the Hospice was carrying around their huge, heavy, stuffed gorilla mascot and I had the bright idea of putting him on Cherry Blossom's back and carrying it around that way. Like many ancient mill houses, Runcton is surrounded by water. We rode easily over the bridge across the stream, on to the central island, where the bulk of the people were gathered. However, donkeys notoriously have their peculiarities and are renowned for their obstinacy, and although she had crossed over the little bridge Cherry Blossom refused to cross back again. She is overweight and floppy-bellied and there was nothing we could do to shift her, but I thought that if we brought the always biddable Henry over, she would be bound to follow him back. Wrong – on this occasion Henry also resolutely refused to cross back over the bridge, so we now had two donkeys stuck on the island, and they remained there until the end of the fête. Finally, there was no other solution to the problem except brute force and we enlisted the help of six of the strongest people we could find. With a lot of shoving, swearing and heaving, eventually both donkeys were returned to the other side at last. A sublime example of the stubbornness of asses.

The spring brought new actors, and we were fortunate enough to have Christopher Benjamin living in the annexe while he was starring in Bernard Shaw's *Getting Married*. However, as the three new cats had had the whole annexe to themselves over the winter, Sheba, who could open doors by swinging on the handles, was highly annoyed at the invasion of her territory and started to vent her irritation on Libra, the timid cat, behind the books in the library. The situation grew progressively worse, Libra refused to come down for her food, which I was having to leave on the top shelf, and Sheba started to tear the covers of Patrick's books in her attempts to climb up and get at her.

I kept moving the books around and pushing the valuable ones to the back, but I knew it would be only a matter of time before the damage was discovered – and then all hell would break loose, and not among the cats! It was serious – what the animals were to me, Patrick's books were to him. In fact I found it peculiar that even when he said he was calling a halt to buying more books they still seemed to multiply. I could only presume that books had a secret sex life of their own on the shelves at night for them to proliferate in such large numbers. In the interests of peace something would have to be done about the cat warfare, either Sheba or Libra would have to go. Or, said Patrick, *he* would!

Marilyn the local physiotherapist had just lost her own cat on the Selsey road. This was instantly reported to me. Libra I knew was the ideal cat as she would not go very far and kind Marilyn was persuaded to take her on. Libra departed happily for her new home, and serenity and tranquillity returned to ours.

13

The Dove that Loved Ducks and the Lady that Wanted Love

When Patrick offered me the part of Rachel Wardle in the musical *Pickwick* with Harry Secombe and Roy Castle, which he was directing at Chichester, I leapt at the idea. Not only would my salary pay for new post-and-rail fencing to help keep Cherry Blossom and Pepsi in, but I had not danced or sung for some time and to work for Gillian Lynne, the *Cats* choreographer, had always been one of my ambitions. I consulted Jessie and she was perfectly happy to take over while I rehearsed. Once the show was running I was able to be with my animals during the daytime, except on matinée days.

I became extremely fit from all the dancing, got away with the singing (not my forte) and was delighted to play a part in what turned out to be the smash hit of the season.

Once the show was playing I took more notice of what was going on at home and was alarmed to find the hare, who usually had a healthy, shiny coat, looking rather mangy. I took him to the vet.

'You had better wash both Tiney and the guinea-pig in an anti-parasite shampoo,' said the vet.

Back I went and prepared washing-up bowls full of

warm water. Bob the gardener and Brian our American friend, who was sorting out our wild garden, looked on in amazement as I shampooed first Mr Big the guinea-pig and then the hare. Washing the guinea-pig went smoothly enough as he went fairly limp and let me bath and rinse him, but the hare was quite another matter. Whichever way I held him, by the neck, by the ears, by the waist, by the bottom, his strong legs kicked out in all directions, sending suds and water everywhere and overturning the bowls. By the time I had finished I was wet through and my hair hung in lank strands down the sides of my face.

'I've washed my hare, and I can't do a thing with it,' said Brian with his sardonic sense of humour, as Bob and he laughed at my discomfiture.

Unfortunately, the diagnosis was wrong and I noticed that having been a very clean animal, Tiney started leaving messes all over the place and his coat still looked dull while the freshly washed guinea-pig gleamed in the sunlight. Back I went to the vet.

'We'll give him antibiotics and vitamin shots,' said the lady vet, 'but I must warn you these may be signs of myxomatosis and they rarely recover.'

I was dumbstruck. 'How can a pet hare that never sees another rabbit possibly get myxomatosis?'

'Easy – the disease is carried by fleas, I'm afraid,' she said. 'Even a rabbit that lives indoors can get it. You needed a vaccination against it.'

I took poor Tiney home with a heavy heart, and sure enough, her prognosis was correct and slowly the beautiful hare-rabbit deteriorated.

Eventually we couldn't bear to watch his suffering any longer and the vet put him down humanely. Dear Tiney now resides next to Sophie, Kipling, Ben and Whitey in our little copse by the annexe.

There were casualties in the poultry world also. One

day I spotted a young Silkie hen staggering around like a drunk and decided to take her to the vet. Jessie opted to come with me for which I was grateful. Once at the surgery the vet diagnosed a middle-ear infection. 'I'll give her an injection now and one of you will have to put the needle into her breast-bone every day for a week,' she said. 'Also she'll need to be kept very warm.'

Fortunately Jessie didn't blanch at the thought and said she would be the injection giver.

Back home, after much deliberation, Jessie and I decided to install Viviana (I'd named the hen after the dancer Viviana Durante) in the spare bathroom above the kitchen with its permanently warm Aga. We lined the bath with newspapers, put in a cardboard box full of straw for her bed, and bowls of water and vitamin-enriched food. The warmth and the antibiotic shots seemed to work and she grew stronger by the day.

One afternoon an actor friend, Keith Baxter, called on us and decided to pay a visit to that particular bathroom without alerting me. Suddenly there was a loud squawk followed by a muffled scream as Keith fled downstairs hardly pausing to adjust his apparel!

'Not many people keep hens in their bath,' he stuttered. 'You might have warned me!'

Unfortunately, when we put Viviana back with her family outside she rapidly went down hill and this time nothing could save her. A local farmer said to me one day: 'When you keep poultry, you must expect the odd death now and then, you know.'

I understood, but somehow I always knew the personalities of my birds so well that they were more like pets, like cats or dogs, and I always fought for their lives in just the same way.

My duck population always fluctuated and I have yet to find anyone who can tell me for how long ducks live;

all the books say 'prepare for table' which is not my idea of duck-keeping at all. Certainly amongst my Aylesbury population eight appears to be old. I had added tiny Call ducks, bantam Silver Appleyards, large brown and white Rouen ducks and Buff Orpington ducks, but it was the Indian Runners that always gave me the most pleasure. I had a black Indian Runner sitting on a nest of eggs in the coop while her black Indian Runner sister ran around outside. One day the one outside went missing and I came to the conclusion that Mr Fox must have passed by in the daytime and appropriated her. However, on checking the coop where the black Indian Runner sat on eggs, I could make out the dark shape of another duck behind. It was the dead body of the one who had been sitting on the eggs. Her sister, seeing what had happened, had moved her off the nest and sat on the eggs herself. Unfortunately, the ducklings never did hatch, the eggs must have chilled before the 'aunt' discovered her sister had died, but that Indian Runner certainly showed presence of mind.

After years of duck-keeping the only way to achieve success in duckling rearing appears to be to isolate the duck and her nest to stop her adding other eggs to it and to concentrate her mind on the sitting so she doesn't leave the nest for very long. Even so, when hatched, there are still perils: magpies, crows, rooks and rats love a juicy duckling if they wander loose. It is best to house them in a separate rabbit hutch with a closed run, double wired on all sides, and keep them there until they are large enough to brave the outside world.

I witnessed another example of the caring nature of ducks in a pair of elderly Rouen ducks, a brown drake and a white duck. The poor drake went blind and his wife/partner would lead him around the paddock each day and in the evening would guide him back to the food and water in the aviary. They were a devoted couple.

One day my birds' peace was shattered when some-one dumped a vagrant guinea-fowl amongst them – a guinea-fowl that made my vicious one seem like a cuddly teddy bear. It chased all the ducks and hens all day long and finally pecked out the eyes and killed the poor blind Rouen drake. His white Rouen wife remained a sad, solitary figure, and the murderous guinea-fowl was banished to the wilds of the Norton Priory Woods. When last seen it was being chased by another guinea-fowl and a peacock. Serves it right.

Jessie has six children, but the only ones I know well are her two daughters Linda and Sue, aged twenty-seven and twenty-two, attractive, strong girls like their mother, and animal lovers too. Sue still lives with her parents Jessie and John, and has managed to persuade them to share their immaculate house with two rottweilers, an alsatian and one of my rescued cats, Tosca (son of Camilla, my grey Rex-Chinchilla). She also has two horses, which she keeps at the stables where she works.

Linda, by virtue of living in a small house with her husband Neil, has less room, but none the less manages to co-habit with two dogs, rabbits and guinea-pigs. She also keeps two horses at her friend Mona Joyce's and has a full-time job working for the Finnish Spitz breeders, travelling with them to dog shows around the country.

One day Linda turned up at Poplars with a small white dove she had found at work. 'It's a bit sick and it can't fly, but I thought you would know what to do with it,' she said.

'It may be a candidate for Dennis Fenter's Bird Hospital, but let's have a look at it first,' I said, and examined it gently. There appeared to be nothing broken although it was clearly very unwell.

'It may just be exhausted and hungry. We can put it in

the spare outdoor cage, give it mixed corn and water and keep it under observation,' I said.

Linda agreed and, sure enough, within a week the little dove had recovered and was flying happily from perch to perch, in perfect health. Now I was in the same dilemma I had been in with Mr Pigeon, and I knew that this bird, being an ordinary dove, would not find its way home. Also, I didn't want it back in the place where it had got so ill, in case of a recurrence.

Two weeks had passed with the dove in solitary isolation when Jessie's other daughter Sue and her fiancé Jason turned up at the door.

'We've brought you a present,' said Sue grinning. 'We were at an animal fair and couldn't resist them – Patrick isn't around, is he?' she added, looking about her anxiously. I said he wasn't and on that they produced two tiny white calling-ducks from a cardboard box, very pretty and fluffy and making the repetitive siren noise that only calling-ducks can. This meant they were ducks, not drakes – the male merely squeaks softly – which was a relief as too many males always resulted in battered ducks. Besides, I had a calling drake already; he had married a Khaki Campbell female. The reason I had only one small duck left was that they are 'flighty' if they are tiny, weighing so little that they fly off, so the new call ducks were going to pose a problem.

'I'm not worried about Patrick,' I said. 'The fact that the ducks are a gift means that *I* can't be held to blame! And he can't be cross with *you* for being so generous. Besides, what are another two ducks when you already have forty?' (Although, frankly, I doubt that my logic would have convinced Patrick.)

I then explained that they would have to be kept in for the statutory six weeks until they regarded Poplars as their home, at the end of which I would clip their wings as an added precaution. The wing feathers would eventually grow again, but by then they would be at home, and unlikely to wander.

We looked around and decided that the best place to keep them was in the cage with the solitary white dove. The dove immediately flew down to join the two little white ducks and did a little dance of pleasure, hopping from leg to leg, ruffling its feathers and billing and cooing at them. The ducks looked rather surprised, but it was the dove's territory so they decided that they had better be polite. As a result, the dove stopped living on the perches and spent its entire time on the ground with them eating the same corn and maize, sleeping in the same hutch, and sitting on the edge of the washing-up bowls while they bathed.

Finally the six weeks were up and the time came to trim the ducks' wings and release them on to the pond with the others. The problem was going to be the little dove, but he was so fond of his webbed-footed friends that I suspected he would try and stay close to them and hoped that any lurking cat would think he was another small white Silkie hen! Jessie and I let the call ducks out, and as we'd expected the little dove pottered about after them. In fact, much to our amazement he followed them religiously all day long. He had trouble keeping up with them on the pond, so spent a fair bit of time either up to his knees in water at the edge of the pond, or anxiously watching them on the tiny island in the middle of it. All three were accepted by the resident duck population, but as usual, Goosey, the greylag, who knows each member of her duck family, tried to shoo away the newcomers. They were able to dodge her, though, and by the end of the day she seemed to accept them.

That evening Jessie and I mounted a strategic pincer movement to get the two new ducks back into their anti-fox cage and much to our astonishment the little dove flew over, landed and walked in too, obviously very chuffed that his two pals were finally back on dry land. After a few days the letting-out and putting-in routine was established; every day the little dove would follow his duck friends round and round the pond, and at dusk he would follow them into their cage, joining them in their straw-lined hutch for the night. However, one day after a great deal of torrential rain the pond turned into a lake and flooded right into the calling ducks' cage, although not into their hutch, which was up on bricks to prevent damp. That night as Jessie and I put them away, the floodwater proved to be quite a problem for the little dove. He had always landed on the ground and walked in with the ducks and on this occasion he couldn't do so. At first we tried to propel him in with long poles, but he would simply fly off and sit on top of the cage. We then tried fishing nets in an attempt to catch him, but all to no avail, he simply could not fly straight in through the open door. As darkness fell we were obliged to give up, and we left him looking dejected on top of his friends' cage.

The following morning there was no sign of the little dove and we feared the worst; he would never have left his two duck pals, and they called forlornly for their tiny friend all day. In the evening we discovered the two ducks in a corner looking at a few white feathers – they had found what remained of their little friend. It would not have been the cats, they would never have gone through the water, but that cunning Mr Fox had been around looking for his dinner again. We were more upset over the demise of the little dove than we'd have expected.

'I'll get you another one if you like,' said Linda, very kindly, but I politely declined. You don't get a white dove falling in love with call ducks every day.

There were other bird problems. I had begun to find our post thrown over the gate with 'geese loose' scrawled on it. The geese were such sweet, gentle creatures, waggling their heads up and down, nibbling your fingers and holding long conversations with you, there had to be some mistake. Why, only the previous week Jock the postman had said he much preferred the dobermanns to the guinea-fowl, and I had pointed out the stick by the gate, used for guinea-fowl control. Obviously the new postman couldn't tell a guinea-fowl from a goose.

Shortly afterwards, however, I had occasion to call in two young thatchers as the annexe roof was leaking. After they had finished examining the decayed reeds we returned to the front of the house.

'We'll send you an estimate next week,' the tall Master Thatcher said.

Meanwhile my inquisitive Canada geese, Bill and Ben, had, as usual, come to investigate what was going on and were examining their tools.

The Master Thatcher, 6 foot 4 inches tall, leant to pick up his bag, towering over the goose, and suddenly, as he turned to go, Ben attacked him hissing and threshing his wings. I intervened and Ben stopped in his tracks, but meanwhile the second young man had panicked and bolted down the drive with Bill firmly attached to his bottom. He vaulted over the five-bar gate and Bill was forced to let go of his trousers.

By now safe in his truck, the Master Thatcher collapsed in stitches at the sight of his friend, a fully grown man, being chased by a mere goose. I would have been just as amused had it not begun to dawn on me that I had another problem on my hands. The postman had been right after all – our vicious guinea-fowl was only knee high, these savage Canada geese were aiming below the belt! No longer tender down-covered goslings, they had turned into fully fledged cantankerous adolescents.

Clip their wings again? We couldn't wait for their flight feathers to grow back.

Three days later Jessie was appalled when she went to put the birds away and discovered four Canada geese on the pond with the greylag. She thought I had played a terrible trick and acquired some more without telling her. Fortunately, when she tried to herd them into their rather cramped quarters, two of them flew away. I like to think it was one of our original nursery geese that had come to show off its mate to us and to his old chums.

Goosey, the greylag, remained her good-natured self and we were all excited when she laid her first huge egg in the gardener's green Bos-bag while he was weeding the wildflower bank, even though we knew it would be infertile. I'm afraid we sold it to Munneries, the local greengrocer's for sixty pence.

The adventures of the geese had to be curtailed, and Jim arrived once again, armed with chicken wire to nail to the post-and-rail fencing to keep the geese to the confines of the pond and paddock. As our grown-up geese had now become the self-appointed guardians of Poplars Farm House, when we were not expecting visitors we would, however, often open their gate and let them roam. After all, the ferocious dobermann pinschers wouldn't say boo to a goose!

There was another animal whose movements had to be curtailed as well and that was Daisy, the dobermann. While I was working so hard on *Pickwick* which, with all the dancing, was exhausting, Patrick volunteered, at least on matinée days, to walk the dogs for me. It was good exercise for him and afforded him a moment's relaxation.

With Daisy's mania for hunting, when you took her for a walk you had to call her back regularly to keep her near, otherwise she would disappear into the distance. The trouble with Patrick in his job as Artistic Director was that he was always so preoccupied with the running of the theatre and with his creative thoughts that he could never concentrate long on the reality of what was happening about him.

I therefore advised Patrick to let Dorrit roam, but to keep Daisy firmly on the lead. Absentmindedly, he let her off and she went missing for forty-eight hours. We advertised on the local radio and in the newspapers, and eventually there came news of a sighting of her several miles away, near a caravan park at Selsey Bill. Patrick was so relieved to see her back, he hadn't the heart to reproach her. When we got Daisy home she could hardly walk, her foot pads were raw, and she didn't move from her basket for twenty-four hours.

Chastened, Patrick then became more careful, but one day, on the stretch home and feeling sorry for her, he let her off the lead again. Daisy, followed by Dorrit, promptly vanished into the middle distance in pursuit of a dozen enticing scents; Patrick, yelling vainly, blundered along miles behind, until both dogs were out of sight.

My whole day before the show in the evening was spent motoring for hours down remote tracks not meant for cars, all to no avail. Finally, Jessie and her husband went looking and Linda volunteered to go out on her horse. She eventually found Dorrit in the road at Pagham, and Daisy appeared exhausted from the foul bottom of a ditch. They stank revoltingly and had to be bathed before they could collapse on to their beds once again. This time the pads of their feet were worn to shreds and it took several days for them to heal.

More man-hours had been spent finding the dogs than Patrick had spent walking them. He was mortified and so apologetic that it meant that when I had a phone call about a young dobermann that needed a home, Patrick was not really in a strong position to refuse her!

*

The call came from a warm-hearted lady called Gladys Roberts, who had had two rescued Rex cats from me. They had been difficult to home as one had a bad eye and the other had had her jaw broken in an accident, but it didn't bother Gladys, she took them just the same. This time she was asking me to help her. 'It's a matter of some urgency – could you possibly take on a young black-and-tan dobermann bitch, called Lady?' she asked. 'She's a sweet dog.'

It wasn't exactly the best moment. *Pickwick* was about to transfer to London, but I certainly couldn't turn down an eighteen-month-old dobermann and at least we had a week off from the play prior to moving to Sadler's Wells Theatre.

'Where is she?' I asked.

The next day found me knocking on the door of a caravan at Bognor. A black-and-tan dobermann bounded through the door and nearly knocked me over; she was the image of Kipling, but took your wrist in her mouth like Blue. I looked into her deep brown winsome eyes and was lost.

Her owner was a lorry driver who was away working for very long hours. 'She destroys the place while I'm out, makes messes and wants to play when I get home,' he said. For some reason he was surprised that an adolescent dobermann cooped up in a tiny space for hours on end could behave so irresponsibly.

I had to do something and, as a temporary solution, offered to collect her each morning, walk her with Daisy and Dorrit, feed her, and return her exhausted each evening. I couldn't take her to Poplars, only to leave her a week later, and it would give me time to assess the situation.

It took me three days to love her as, after months of neglect, she responded to care and attention with a heart-

rending devotion. She wouldn't leave my side. The problem was that if you did disappear from her sight
she would panic, and jump out of windows and climb
eight-foot walls to get to you. I thought the answer
would be to leave her in the car when I couldn't be with
her. It was an expensive idea – in fifteen minutes she ate
through two seat belts.

The frustrating thing was that I knew Lady would be
an ideal dog with time spent on her, but I didn't have that
time, I was off to London. However, I didn't want to lose
her, I decided to talk to Patrick. 'Darling,' I said, 'there's
a young black-and-tan dobermann bitch, like Kipling,
that needs a home. What is more, she sticks to you like
superglue so even you wouldn't be able to lose her.'

I knew, after Patrick's recent disasters with Daisy, I
was in a powerful position, and sure enough he capitul-
ated: 'Well, we could try,' he answered reluctantly.

This, however, was not the whole answer: the more I
got to know Lady with her paranoia at being left behind,
the more I realized that, even with Patrick's agreement, I
still had to find a solution. The ever-tolerant Jessie would
hand in her notice if she were left alone to cope with
Lady. I would have to take her with me to London.
When I thought of our recently decorated apartment I
feared what she might do to it while I was at the theatre
each evening, and even if I could confine her I knew she
would howl the place down and there were other residents to think of. I thought I had the answer when a
dobermann breeder friend offered to lend me a dog cage
for the back of my car, but it wasn't to be. Patrick
wanted to take my hatchback to Corsica, leaving me his
Mercedes saloon. The cage wouldn't fit on his back seat
and what she would do to his cherished car in three
hours I dreaded to think.

The only answer was for Sue, Jessie's daughter, to

agree to walk Lady each day along with Daisy and Dorrit, not to mention her two rottweilers and alsatian. She willingly came to the rescue, but three days after I arrived in London she rang me at Sadler's Wells Theatre in a panic.

'I've spoken to the man's next-door neighbour – he beats Lady, he was even reported to the RSPCA. You've got to get her away from him.'

'Sue, I'm in London, I can't deal with this, I can't inflict Lady on your mother, she's got quite enough to cope with as it is without a paranoid dobermann.'

But Sue had another suggestion: 'My friend, the dog-trainer, will have her.'

It did seem like an excellent idea at the time, and I agreed that Sue should take her and board Lady with the experienced dog-trainer.

Two days later, just before I was due to go on stage for the opening night of *Pickwick*, I had another desperate call from Sue.

'The dog-trainer can't cope with Lady, she's howling so much the neighbours are threatening to report him, he wants her to go this evening.'

I rang home immediately. 'Jessie, I'm sorry to have to ask you this, but the dog-trainer has asked Sue to take Lady away tonight. I'm stuck here so I can't help, the only place she knows is Poplars, so please will you tell Sue you will look after her tonight. Meanwhile I'll think of something.'

Jessie is one of those exceptional human beings who always comes up trumps in a crisis. 'All right,' she said. 'So long as it's just for tonight.'

'By the way,' I said, 'if you want to get any sleep I suggest you let Lady sleep on your bed, that's what she's used to.'

'Thanks a lot,' said Jessie.

In the event Lady, who was exhausted by the stress of the previous two days, and Jessie both slept like logs. I didn't sleep at all, I had to come up with an answer.

At 8.30 a.m. I was on the phone to my unflappable friend Liz, at Dobermann Rescue in Portsmouth. I explained the situation and she sweetly offered to fetch Lady herself and look after her until I returned to Chichester – 'I am, after all, the expert on lunatic dobermanns,' she said.

I rang Liz daily from London for reports.

On Tuesday: 'She got into the sink today and tried to get out of the kitchen window to join me.'

On Wednesday: 'She climbed on to the oven and ate the hot casserole.'

On Friday: 'She climbed over the stable door into the dining room and scratched all the paint off the walls.'

I was worried about the damage but Liz cheerfully admitted that 'There wasn't too much paint left, other dobermanns had clawed it off before Lady.' She also agreed that Lady was very lovable although, she said, 'For the moment her manners leave a little to be desired.'

Liz was very happy to keep her on and even advocated it as she thought she would improve under her guidance. My black-and-tan dobermann was safe for the moment. I was still worried, though, as there was to be only a two-week break before the musical transferred to Birmingham, and Jessie had agreed that I should go with it.

It was while I was wondering about how best to cope with Lady and Birmingham that Sue rang me very excitedly: 'I've found a wonderful home for Lady with my hairdresser,' she said.

I didn't want to part with Lady but I knew, as with my cat rescue, that I had to do what was best for the dog, not for me.

I called Marianne, Sue's hairdresser: 'Lady's a sweet

dog, but paranoid about being left, and that's a big problem – she'll do anything, and I mean *anything* to be with you.'

Marianne laughed. 'First, she would never be left on her own, as my husband and I live with my parents, so there's always someone at home, and secondly, the male dobermann we rescued bites people and often runs away – in comparison Lady's perfect.' I had to admit to myself that Marianne did sound right for Lady and it wasn't fair to ask Dobermann Rescue to foster her for another three months. Liz volunteered to bring Lady over the first Sunday I was back from London, and Marianne agreed to come over with Major, her dobermann, to see how they got on.

When Lady arrived she grabbed hold of my wrist ecstatically and pulled me round in circles she was so excited to see me. Daisy and Dorrit were less than thrilled at the return of their lunatic friend, and Major was enchanted at being amongst three beautiful girl dobermanns. After a long walk to tire them all out, during which neither Major or Daisy ran away, I agreed that Marianne should take Lady home.

I rang first thing next morning, but all was well. 'The two dogs played non-stop,' Marianne reported. 'There was one awkward moment when Major woke up, and he growled at finding Lady still here, but the tension passed and they started playing again.'

A week later not only was Major not growling, but he was so entranced with Lady that he had even stopped running away and at night they curled up together. For a while Lady's appalling table manners persisted as she climbed on to all accessible work surfaces, cupboards and tables to get at the food. 'But,' said Marianne cheerfully, 'we've learned the secret is to put everything away.'

Lady's panic attacks also continued for a while and

once, finding herself separated from Marianne who had gone into the garden, instead of going downstairs Lady took the shortest route to join her: she mounted the dressing table and took a flying leap out of the first-floor window, scattering makeup and ornaments in all directions.

I had warned Marianne and her husband, Gordon, about the car, so when they went shopping for half an hour with Lady in their Land-Rover they went prepared and left a large chewy bone to keep her occupied. When they returned they had difficulty opening the car door as Lady had clawed the interior to tatters; of the passenger seat there was no sign, it had been demolished. Gordon, however, showed remarkable sang-froid and continued to take Lady out in his car; now whenever he has to leave her alone, he simply takes the one remaining seat, the driver's seat, with him. More devoted owners could not have been found – as they said of her previous owner: 'That was no way to treat a Lady.'

14

Mr Pickwick, Mr Cardy
and the Norfolk Blacks

The actress Susan Hampshire (who is married to the
Greek producer and shipowner, Sir Eddie Kulakoundis)
once remarked that if you lived with a high achiever you
were likely to be knocked over by his wake. It was certainly true of life with the Artistic Director of the
Chichester Festival Theatre. Patrick was under so much
stress, overseeing past productions, creating the present
ones and meeting famous actors about future plays, not
to mention running the theatre on a daily basis, that the
pressures inevitably rubbed off on me as well. And I
thought, naively, that getting away from Chichester and
going on tour, where I would have only myself to think
about, would be something of a holiday. Jessie and her
husband John had agreed to move into the annexe apartment temporarily and would look after all the animals,
and Patrick, in my absence.

How misguided I was. To be rehearsing in a musical is
like being an Olympic athlete, you have to be on top
form, and it was a lot more tiring than looking after
Patrick, cleaning out all the animals and dog-walking
every day. Also, none of us could have foreseen the
extraordinary events that lay ahead.

Besides finding a home for Lady I was also constantly
finding homes for cats and, just before I was due to leave
for Birmingham I heard of a ten-year-old white Grand

Champion Rex that needed a home. He had been passed from breeder to breeder after the death of his owner and was in a pretty sorry state both psychologically and physically. The dobermanns had to stay behind and guard Poplars and I knew I would miss my animals in the three months I would be on tour in Birmingham; I determined to take the cat with me. Since the death of Whitey I had always had a soft spot for white cats, but more important I was sure that of the twenty-six people working on *Pickwick* someone would want to give him a home.

I had taken a small cottage on a farm outside Birmingham, sharing with the actors Robert Meadmore and Peter Land. Neither they nor the landlord had any objection to my little feline companion, so Patrick and I set off up North with him in a carrier in the back of my car. The trip was quiet and uneventful but once we arrived at our destination his Rex vocal chords let rip. Patrick was rather sympathetic about the poor cat's disorientation: 'It's rather like you or me being put down in the centre of Birmingham,' he said, thinking no doubt of the notorious Spaghetti Junction, and indeed it was very muddling, as we tried to find our way to the theatre around the city's one-way system next morning. However, the cat soon regained his composure as he luxuriated on the mini electric blanket I had bought for him and played with his unfamiliar toys. He seemed not to know his name – Bonnie – which seemed a stupid name for such a distinguished boy, so instead I called him Cardy after David Cardy who played Sam Weller so brilliantly in the show, and also because, with his Rex coat, he looked like an Aran cardigan.

Pickwick the musical was a smash hit at the Birmingham Alexandra Theatre, the box office took over a million pounds in advance bookings and we had

'House Full' signs up at every show. The audience adored Sir Harry and Roy. It is lovely to be appreciated and we were a very happy company indeed, full of vitality and high spirits. Cardy, too, had adjusted to our theatrical hours with the help of Hodge's battery-powered cat-food timer bowl, rearranging his toys in our absence and purring away happily when we were at home.

However, in the theatre, on a long tour, it is rare for everything to remain on an even keel and by the end of December a savage flu bug was going around the company. When there are so many actors singing in such close contact the germs get passed on very easily. I succumbed after New Year's Eve and developed the worst cough I have ever had. The local doctor diagnosed flu exacerbated by a bacterial lung infection brought on by the dusty conditions. For a week I stayed in bed at the cottage in Birmingham, on steroids, antibiotics and inhalers.

Meanwhile there were more dramas back home in Chichester, exaggerated by the sensational news reports from the media. The River Lavant had burst its banks and flooded the city and many areas were cut off, Green Goddesses and fire engines were pumping away twenty-four hours a day and it still continued to rain. Lying ill in my bed in Birmingham my condition was, if anything, made worse by the reports from home, particularly as Patrick and Jessie both liked to embellish it.

'The drive is flooded' – 'there's water pouring into the garden' – 'you need wellingtons to get to the car' – 'the water's rising up the side of the hen and duck coops'. The ducks could swim, but the hens couldn't: 'Can't you move them?' I begged down the phone, frustrated at the distance.

'Oh, it's all right,' said the ever-optimistic Jessie, 'I'm monitoring the situation.'

I wasn't remotely reassured and tossed and turned that night having nightmares about drowning chickens and guinea-fowl. I even imagined my priceless koi carp floating down the drive. I asked the Birmingham doctor if I could go home.

'Only if you don't try to come back soon, if you come back before you're better, you will be in real trouble,' he said.

Fortunately the girl who lived in the cottage next door volunteered to look after Cardy while I was away, although I had a moment's trepidation when I found out her boyfriend was a taxidermist! Back at home things were bad, but somehow just being in the middle of the situation made it less frightening. The ducks and geese loved the new 'lake', the hens hadn't drowned, and the poor donkeys were up to their knees in mud, when they weren't in their stables or the pigsties, looking thoroughly gloomy. Finally my Chichester doctor pronounced me well enough to return to Birmingham, albeit with an inhaler at the ready and on Monday 17 January I was back on stage. By the Friday, for reasons I could never have foreseen, Cardy the cat and I were back in Chichester.

I had returned to a happy company, pleased to have me back, with 'House Full' signs as usual at the front of house and very appreciative audiences, who always gave Roy Castle, who was receiving chemotherapy for his lung cancer during the run, a huge emotional round of applause. Roy was such a heroic character and much loved by everyone, every week he would leave us all a present of chocolates in our dressing rooms, always giving me Bournville because he remembered that plain chocolate was the only kind I ate. Harry Secombe would buy us champagne regularly, so we were very spoilt!

I have to admit that I was aware that things were slightly wrong in the state of Denmark as neither Gillian

Lynne or Patrick, nor the authors, had been paid and the Chichester Theatre was still owed a vast amount of money by the producer, but nothing had prepared me for what was to come.

As we arrived for the Wednesday matinée one of the actors said that he had heard on the radio that morning that the Alexandra Theatre, owned by the Birmingham City Council, had gone bankrupt. Rumours abounded and in the interval Bernie, Sir Harry Secombe's driver, announced that they had shut down the box office. At the end of our successful matinée the tannoy crackled backstage: the entire *Pickwick* company and all the staff at the Alex were summoned on stage to meet – the Official Receiver.

The theatre had gone bankrupt, he said, they had spent the million-pound advance that *Pickwick* had earned, there was no money in the kitty, and would we please remove our possessions from the dressing rooms. As for the future, all the Equity representative could advise was that the company should apply in writing to the Official Receiver for loss of earnings. The theatre, it turned out, was a charitable trust, and as such no one was responsible for its debts. That night one thousand four hundred people turned up to see the show and found the theatre doors padlocked. Unless they had paid with a credit card (which had insurance) they and the other thousands of people due to see the show in the following weeks lost their money. It was a disgraceful episode.

We were stunned, speechless and angry, particularly when we heard the theatre had tried to blame *Pickwick* for their losses. As we left the theatre I addressed the newsmen congregated at the stage door: 'The musical of *Pickwick* is a smash hit and is not responsible for the losses and debts incurred by the Birmingham Alexandra Theatre,' I said.

Harry Secombe said the same thing when he left, so at least that part of the record was put straight. We were a solid success and would continue to be so in the future.

After the débâcle of that Wednesday we held a wake for the cast at one of our rented cottages on the farm. A lot of pasta was consumed, a great deal of wine was drunk, and a very peculiar time was had by all.

The next day I rang to tell Jessie of my imminent arrival and packed. I felt most sorry for Cardy, the Cornish Rex, who had been so happy in our little cottage and whose idyll had been so summarily disrupted. In the event he settled down at home rather well and was both fearless and non-combative although both Hodge and Coley gave him a hard time.

For about a week all the actors were in constant telephone contact, and we all had the same reaction, we couldn't bring ourselves to unpack and simply stared at our cases. Things were very unsettled, the tour was supposed to go on to Woking, Sheffield and Norwich after finishing in Birmingham. Our set was impounded in the theatre there and the other theatres we heard were trying to negotiate to get it out and get *Pickwick* back on the road. It was a period of great uncertainty and we were all depressed. It seemed inconceivable that such a rich, joyful, and well-received experience in the theatre should turn to ashes in our mouths. But so it did, and the sad demise of *Pickwick* in Birmingham rankled in our minds for a long time. Saying goodbye to Roy Castle was one of the worst moments of this part of the tour, and Patrick and I wondered whether we would ever see him again.

To cheer myself up I decided to ring up Frank Page, the elderly countryman who was a rabbit expert and poultry fancier.

'Frank, it's Alexandra Bastedo, do you remember me?'

'Oh, yes, you're the rabbit lady,' he replied, reminding me of my mistake over Tiney, whom I had inaccurately called a hare. 'What can I do for you?'

'Do you remember when I went to collect some Silkies from Mrs Powell some time ago, you said you might have some Buff Orpington hens for me?' I asked.

'Yes I do,' Frank said, 'and what is more if you want to come over now like, there's a trio ready to go.' I was slightly flustered at the immediacy of the offer, but I had always coveted his birds with their beautiful golden plumage and scarlet red combs, and I determined to strike while the iron was hot.

'Good,' I said, 'but would you mind if I didn't take the cockerel? You see I already have two Silkie cockerels and I don't think the neighbours' – I left out Patrick – 'could stand any more noise.'

'No problem,' said Frank. 'Will two p.m. Tuesday be all right?'

I alerted Jim King who immediately fixed up a large coop with a run by the barn in preparation for their arrival.

At the appointed hour I arrived at Frank's attractive bungalow at Emsworth, and was invited by Queenie, his wife, to tea and homemade shortbread. Frank was no ordinary hen seller, he was a poultry fancier, and as such had to make sure you were worthy of his birds, hence the talk over tea.

As I looked around I remarked upon the various press photographs on the mantelpiece, showing Frank in his cloth cap and tweed jacket holding silver cups with exotic birds or rare rabbits, all covered in rosettes.

'I had no idea Frank, you had won so many awards.' He was rising in my estimation by the minute.

'Oh yes, I bred the first Polish lop-eared dwarf rabbit, who was quite a champion, and those there –' he pointed to some remarkable long-legged birds – 'are my Sumatran gamecock and his hen. They won all the competitions they did.'

'I had no idea you were such an expert,' I said admiringly.

'Oh yes, me and Mr Parr of Hawkley held the first ever poultry fanciers' show at Alexandra Palace. Quite something, that was.'

It would have been very easy to chat to Frank and Queenie all afternoon, but I knew I should settle in my new hens before dusk. 'I really must get back, Frank,' I said, 'I still have to do the animals – are the hens ready?'

'Just a moment,' he replied and one by one fetched in three aerated boxes.

'I thought you said *two* hens,' I remarked.

'I did,' he stated with a mischievous glint in his eyes, 'but I thought you'd be interested to see the cockerel.' With that he opened the largest box and gently pulled out the most beautiful cockerel I had ever seen, honey-coloured, red-crested and with an extravagantly plumed tail which draped in a cascade over his arm. I was speechless.

'He's a beauty, isn't he?' said Frank.

I was lost, of course, as he had anticipated – how could I possibly leave behind this Robert Redford of the cockerel world and deprive two hens of such a handsome husband?

'May I take him too?' I asked weakly. Frank grinned.

'Thought you'd like him if you saw him. Shampooed and blowdried, he'd win any show, he would.'

'I just hope the neighbours can stand an extra cock-a-doodle-doo,' I said.

'Just box him at night, I box all my cock birds,' Frank advised.

I knew this to be the answer, but I also knew from

experience they could get dehydrated during a hot summer; I would have to be cautious.

'Oh, and be careful of his comb,' Frank added, as I put my feathered charges into the car, 'you don't want to damage that.'

Two days later as I charged around with my large koi fishing net trying to get Robert Redford in for the night I was to remember those words. However, I decided that a bruised comb would be a small price for him to pay for not being eaten by Mr Fox, so netted he was.

Finally, much to our delight, the three theatres, Woking, Sheffield and Norwich, who had already sold a lot of *Pickwick* tickets to their audiences, got together a rescue package and bought back our set. Having finished *Pickwick* in Birmingham on such a sorry note of frustration, we were all thrilled to be off on tour again for six weeks, if only to restore the musical's reputation, and we had the marvellous news that Roy Castle was determined to be with us again.

Woking was an easy location for me as it was within commuting distance, which was just as well as serious difficulties developed with the animals. The floods and the mud had taken their toll and one by one the donkeys went down with foot problems. In fact their ailments were so severe, that in the end I had to call in the expert horse vets, Allpress, from Arundel. Foot poultices, antibiotics, pain killers, diet, vitamin supplements, and regular picking out of the hoofs were the instructions, but they said that a lot of equines had suffered from the mud and really they should be kept off it. What was I to do? I had some savings left from *Pickwick* before the Alexandra Theatre went bust, and I resolved to spend them all on creating a large area of concrete hard-standing for the donkeys. A friend of Bob our gardener's rushed over with his digger and cement mixer and, before I left for Sheffield, Henry and his ladies were all happily confined to hard ground, clattering about.

The other problem was Cardy whom I didn't feel I should uproot again. I felt he needed a particular friend as, although he was tolerated by our other cats, I knew without me he would be lonely. However, I knew not of one, but of two cats that needed homes and resolved to put them with Cardy, despite Patrick's passionate protestations. As in my absence they were to live in a room at the back of the house with access to the field, away from Patrick, I hoped they would be no trouble. One cat was a little chocolate and white Rex called Coco and the other a beautiful white female stray called Maisie from Monique's, who would bite your hand gently at meal times, she was so desperate to be fed, and they became Cardy's feline family. Soon Coco was always to be found curled up with Cardy, so all was well.

Once again I left Jessie and John in residence and, after a successful two weeks at Woking, set off for my cottage outside Sheffield on a working farm. What I hadn't realized was that it was a meat farm and that most of the calves and piglets had a twelve-month life span if they were lucky, while with the lambs it was more like fifteen weeks. I longed for former days when sheep were kept mainly for their wool and cows for their milk. However, they were well kept and the lady farmer bemoaned Britain's involvement with the EC, whose regulations, she said, had made things worse for the animals, not better. I knew from my own experience that the EC had removed a lot of animal products from the farm supply shelves and to get round their absence I had been forced to treat my hens for red mites with a budgerigar spray!

As an actress working at night I liked to sleep late in the morning. But with three cockerels crowing beneath my window and the dawn chorus of bleating, mooing and snorting, together with the farm shop and outside telephone bells, I longed for mornings at Poplars Farm House which seemed, in comparison, like a monastic retreat.

At Norwich I was to stay on another farm in the village of Cringleford, but after the noise at Sheffield I was rather relieved to learn that all the farm buildings had been converted into cottages, at least they would be quiet, and one could sleep in.

En route to Norwich from Sheffield I decided to drop in on Bob Mann and his wife Patti, who were fellow dobermann owners, but who also owned a parrot farm where they hand-reared baby parrots. Since Sid, the African Grey, had stayed in the annexe I had to admit that I had a penchant for parrots.

I arrived as they were about to serve tea, but, more important, just in time to witness Patti Mann feeding all the baby parrots, which she did every four hours (including through the night). The little parrots – African Greys, four species of cockatoo, six kinds of Amazon and eight types of macaw – were so tiny, bald, with a little patch of down, that they were virtually indistinguishable from each other, but they all ate ravenously before being put back in their heated cages. Patti told me that as they got older they were allowed to roam all over the carpets of the house which meant that their little rescued Fell terrier and dobermann had to be very well disciplined to leave them alone.

In the sitting room there was a pair of exotic Palmes with long beaks, curved like scythes, and incredible mobile crests that fanned out. They were sitting untethered outside their cage. 'They have to be watched though,' said Patti. 'Once I forgot to put them back in their cage when I went out and when I came back we didn't have a skirting board left.'

Tea was shared with a twelve-month-old female cockatoo who loved nothing better than to share a scone, and she would sit on your shoulder, softly nibbling your ear, preening your hair, and making affectionate cooing noises, although the appearance of anyone new would inspire an ear-splitting squawk. I asked Bob about the best way to keep such an exotic bird.

'I would be very sad if any bird of mine spent all day in a cage,' he said. 'They are all such personalities that they should be enjoyed, like cats or dogs, and given a certain amount of freedom.'

To round off the visit Bob took me to look round his vast, airy aviaries full of his own older, and rescued birds; when they saw him, two rainbow-coloured macaws arrived on his shoulder and smothered him with kisses. The other birds all wanted to embrace their 'daddy' as well, but were kept off by the two macaws. These birds were all spectacular with a huge variety of colours to their plumage and I longed to know more about them with a view to the future. 'Are there any problems with parrot-keeping?' I asked.

'The only thing we ever had trouble with,' Bob said, 'was the water. The fledglings were dying and we traced the problem to the local water supply which had too many nitrites, nitrates and chlorides.' He recommended bottled water; but even then, he said, you have to check the labels, as the quality varies enormously.

I would have loved to have shared my supper too with the resident cockatoo, but I had to tear myself away from Bob, Patti and the parrots and head on to Norwich. However, if I had been homeward bound to Poplars instead I rather fear I might have been driving south with an Amazon, a macaw, an African Grey, or a cockatoo on my shoulder. As it was I arrived at my Cringleford village cottage birdless.

Norwich is not only one of the most beautiful cities of a thousand churches but it is also surrounded by heavenly countryside, full of all sorts of animal sanctuaries and breeding centres. When Patrick, as our director, came up to check on *Pickwick*, we took some time off to visit the Rare Breeds Centre near Cromer. How I coveted the Pygmy goats, the Jacob sheep, the Dexter cattle and the Norfolk turkeys. I got into deep conversation with Alex Loads, the owner, a fair-haired cheerful woman, who offered me one of Samantha the Iron Age pig's offspring – Patrick intervened, but not before I had persuaded her to take on some rare Cornish Rex cats to keep down the unwelcome rats in their food barn!

While away I telephoned Jessie regularly for news: the donkeys' feet were better, Cardy and his friends were fine, Daisy and Dorrit had not been lost, Bob the gardener had accidentally colour-co-ordinated the brown and white hens and cockerels one night when he had put them to bed which had mixed up the Silkie families and caused quite a rumpus, and, lastly and sadly, one of the two guinea-fowl had died. It was the quiet, sweet one that had passed away, probably of old age, and everyone except me regretted that it wasn't the vicious one. However, my favourite, whether George or Georgina, was the malevolent bird with whom I had a peculiarly loving friendship. I alone had never been attacked, (except when I was in high heels and evening dress and was unrecognizable) and he/she would spend hours in a submissive position being stroked by me – I would have missed that guinea-fowl even more than its friend.

With Patrick safely back at Chichester I made enquiries locally about Norfolk turkeys, which are considered to be a rare breed, and was directed to Thuxton, where James Graham, of Peele's Norfolk Black turkeys lived at Rookery Farm.

I had always been fascinated by turkeys ever since I had read of their suitability as park birds; they are able to roost in trees like peacocks, but they are a lot less noisy. The poor old white turkeys, battery-reared in their thousands, are not suitable as they have been raised for the table, and in later life their legs have difficulty in supporting their weight. The Norfolk turkeys have not been tampered with and remain agile, healthy birds; a glorious colour of black and bronze in the sunlight.

When I arrived at Rookery Farm I spied a handsome, ruddy-faced young man with his sheepdog coming towards me across a field.

'You the lady that wants to see the turkeys?' he asked, warned by my telephone call.

'Yes, but they are real Norfolk Black turkeys, aren't they?' I said, not wanting any hybrids.

'They most definitely are,' he replied. 'In the 1920s they were almost extinct, an old lady had just six, but my grandfather got a trio of baby turkeys from her and he was instrumental in re-establishing the breed again.'

'Does that mean you have lots of them?' I asked.

'Not really, we're just a small enterprise. Besides, all the supermarkets want white turkeys – nobody complains if there's a white feather, but they don't like a black one, and they are bred for their breasts so they can hardly stand up, they're no use as pets if that's what you're wanting.'

I assured him that it was the Norfolk Blacks I was after as I certainly *did* want a pet and he invited me to put on some rather large wellingtons to tramp through the mud.

'We've thirty stags, male birds, each with five hens, but

to get to see them we have to cross this waterlogged field. Follow me.'

Halfway across the meadow my mobile phone went off in my handbag – it was Patrick from Chichester. Mr Graham, the farmer, kept walking.

'Sorry, I can't talk now, I'm in the middle of a bog about to see some Norfolk Black turkeys,' I said. 'Talk to you later.'

'Just don't come back with one,' Patrick said warily and hung up.

As we approached a long corrugated shed that looked like an iron train, the sound of 'gobble, gobble, gobble' started up and echoed back and forth in waves the whole length of the building.

Each family had its own immaculate compartment of clean straw with a couple of bales on the floor and wooden perches for them to roost on. 'Though,' remarked Mr Graham, 'the stag is often so big he falls off.'

The straw bales were for the turkey hens to lay their eggs behind. 'They're rather bad mothers, I'm afraid, so we collect the eggs and raise them in the incubators ourselves.'

'My guinea-fowl book says that turkeys are very stupid and that you need keets [baby guinea-fowl] to teach them what to do,' I said.

Mr Graham laughed: 'You'll find they're not stupid at all. In fact, if they know there's food in the kitchen you'll find them tapping at your door.'

'Since we already have the geese, the guinea-fowl, the hens and Khaki Campbell ducks assembling by the boiler it is going to be a bit crowded,' I said.

I looked into each unit and particularly admired one stag that was exquisite, half bronze and half black, he resembled a peacock when he displayed and his tail fanned out into a myriad of shimmering plumes.

'Could he father my turkey?' I asked.

'Of course,' said Mr Graham, 'but the other thing you will need are turkey saddles to protect the hens from his claws in the mating season.'

I reflected that I really needed some for my beautiful Buff Orpington hens as well. Sometimes my randy Robert Redford cockerel was a bit over-enthusiastic and shredded their feathers. Their carnal appetites were seemingly insatiable, and Patrick always maintained the moral behaviour of our birds was reprehensible in the extreme.

'What about illnesses?' I asked.

'They're peculiar things, turkeys. If they get ill they tend not to give you much notice, they just keel over and die. However, if you do spot blackhead or coccidiosis you can put powdered aureomycin in their water, but you have to act fast.' Apart from that he recommended as food chick crumbs for the young ones and pheasant pellets for the older ones.

Back in the farmhouse kitchen with a welcome kettle brewing on the old Aga the negotiations began.

'How much is a turkey?' I asked, suspecting that Patrick was not entirely averse to *a* turkey.

'A stag and two hens would be the happiest combination,' he replied. 'You could have some early June then they can spend the whole summer and autumn in the open, adjusting to a life outside. As for the price, a ticket to the last night of *Pickwick* wouldn't go amiss.'

The deal was struck, although I knew I would have to rely upon Harry Secombe's intervention to get a ticket as our final week in Norwich was sold out. Back at the theatre Harry promised to obtain one for Mr Graham and at seven o'clock the mobile phone rang again. It was Patrick.

'You haven't got a turkey in your dressing room?' he said.

'Stranger things have happened,' I replied, remembering the time when Jean Boht and I had two Rex cats in our dressing room at the Chichester Theatre. 'But actually, no, I haven't.' At least for that moment I had a clear conscience!

The last night of *Pickwick*, which Patrick returned for, proved to be a very emotional experience for us all. Not only was it the final night of a very successful and happy tour, but all of us watched Roy Castle's last performance from the wings hardly able to control our tears. His courage impressed and moved us all. We were aware how ill he frequently was, and yet 'Doctor Theatre' worked wonders, and he performed with as much energy as ever. He never played below his best. At the curtain call Harry Secombe led him forward and the audience went wild, giving them both a standing ovation. By then most of the cast were openly weeping, it was a night we would never, ever forget. This was Roy's last night on stage, and possibly he was aware of it too. As we said our goodbyes at the stage door, Roy said confidentially to Patrick: 'Here, there's a clause in my contract you don't know about. When I get better, you can fire me.'

The end of the *Pickwick* tour coincided with Patrick's decision to give up the Artistic Directorship of the Chichester Festival Theatre after two terms of four years each. I drove home with him from Norwich with mixed emotions: sadness at the end of such a happy tour, pleasure that it turned out so successfully, delight at the prospect of seeing more of my husband, melancholy at the thought of my deceased guinea-fowl, and longing above all to see my other beautiful animals again.

As I approached the neighbourhood of Poplars Farm House, my anticipation heightened; nor was I to be disappointed: as I arrived at the Sussex gate with its sign BEWARE DOBERMANNS, DONKEYS AND DUCKS, the donkeys brayed their welcome, Goosey shrieked, the ducks quacked and the cockerels joined in with their cock-a-doodle-doo hellos.

My solitary guinea-fowl recognized the car and rushed joyfully towards me and Coley leapt into my lap as I tried to get out, purring his welcome. The dobermanns changed their warning barks to excited whines, and a grinning Patrick opened the front door. I was home at last.

Luis Buñuel, the Spanish film director, was once asked whether he was a true Catholic: 'Probably not,' he said, 'but I have my own religion. Where I am going, *my* heaven will be full of animals.'

In our kitchen, in pride of place, we have a painting full of every kind of creature. Beneath it, handwritten, the Spanish caption reads:

NO HAY PARAISO SIN LOS ANIMALES

'There is no paradise without animals' – for me that simple statement says it all.

Postscript

Remarking on the loneliness of my one remaining guinea-fowl a few days later I decided to visit Mr Hazeldine, a local farmer, who I knew kept guinea-fowl. Obviously what was required was a mate for George or Georgina, but first I needed to know what sex he/she was. Even my guinea-fowl book was very unhelpful, saying how difficult it was to sex them and remarking that sometimes farmers had whole flocks all of males or of females, and wondered why they didn't breed.

In my usual Poplars attire, bare-faced, wind-blown and wearing a mud-spattered anorak and jeans, I encountered a big man with a red complexion coming out of his ramshackle barn, clad in a cloth cap with his trousers held up with bale string. George/Georgina was tucked under my arm.

As I approached him, a large, white, one-legged turkey hopped angrily towards me making a yapping noise like a Jack Russell.

'Oh, don't worry about him,' the man said. 'He's all show, got too big for the oven so the wife decided to keep him as a pet.'

'I'm looking for Mr Hazeldine the farmer,' I said. 'I'm Mrs Garland from Poplars Farm House.'

'I'm Mr Hazeldine –' he paused – 'Poplars Farm House, Poplars Farm House,' he repeated. 'Isn't that where that actress lives with the funny name? Do you know her?'

'You mean Alexandra Bastedo?' I blushed and admitted that I did.

'I suppose she gets you to look after the animals?' he said.

'Yes, you could say that,' I ventured, not wanting to get into deeper water.

I returned to my most pressing problem: 'I've heard you keep guinea-fowl, and wondered if you could sex this one for me.' I proferred George/Georgina and he turned him/her upside-down.

'Well, my dear,' he said after a moment. 'He's a male, I'm ninety per cent sure.'

'Only ninety per cent? Can't you be certain?' I was disappointed.

'Oh no, it's very difficult to distinguish between these here birds, why even farmers have been known to make mistakes.'

He winked. 'An actress would certainly never be able to tell.'

A week later David Bland, a well-known poultry expert, came over to deliver a new hen house. I decided to profit from his visit and consulted him about the gender of my vicious guinea-fowl.

'That's a difficult one,' he said, 'you can get rogue females in the poultry world just as easily as you can in the human race . . . But,' he continued, 'after a great deal of reflection I would say it is ninety per cent sure she's a female. Oh, and by the way, your hens have got scaly leg . . .'

winnebago